BRETHREN NEW TESTAMENT COMMENTARY

HEBREWS

Harold S. Martin

BRF
Published by
Brethren Revival Fellowship
Ephrata, Pennsylvania

ISBN: 978-0-9777766-2-7

Copies of this book are available from:
Brethren Revival Fellowship
P. O. Box 543
Ephrata, PA 17522

GENERAL PREFACE

This commentary is part of a new series of studies that will feature a number of volumes covering all of the New Testament books. There will be reliable expositions of the Bible text, a careful analysis of key words, easy outlines to follow, and helpful material to aid serious Bible students. The explanations are written from a conservative evangelical Brethren and Anabaptist point of view. The goal is to expound the Bible text accurately, and to produce a readable explanation of God's truth.

Each volume can be especially useful for pastors, Sunday School teachers, and lay persons. The writers aim for thoroughness, clarity, and loyalty to the Anabaptist/Pietist values. The meaning of the Greek text (both for those who know Greek and those who don't), will be part of the exposition when necessary.

The *Brethren New Testament Commentary* sponsored by Brethren Revival Fellowship, will simply take the biblical text as it is, and give the exposition along with applications for everyday life. All who have been asked to write the commentaries in this series agree that the message of God's Word in its original documents was given without error, and that nothing more is necessary for spiritual growth.

Brethren Revival Fellowship is a renewal movement within the *Church of the Brethren* which aims to proclaim and preserve biblical values for living today. We believe the Bible is the infallible Word of God, the final authority for belief and practice, and that to personally accept Jesus Christ as Savior is the only means of salvation.

The Brethren Revival Fellowship Committee

This commentary on
the *Book of Hebrews* is affectionately
dedicated to all of our granddaughters.
Their ages range from seven years to thirty years, and include
Rachel Martin (deceased), Lynette Martin (deceased), Jessica
Metzler, Serena Newcomer, Esther Ramer, Jennifer Martin,
Laura Newcomer, Lorinda Newcomer, Lois Ramer, Janelle Martin,
Rosie Newcomer, Dorcas Ramer, Rhoda Newcomer, Janetta
Newcomer, and Rebecca Ramer.
The dedication includes a prayer that each of our granddaughters
will be Proverbs 31 women of God.

FOREWORD

The Brethren New Testament Commentary (the BNTC series) is designed to give a readable explanation of the New Testament text—with loyalty to the Anabaptist and Pietist values. The Anabaptist and Pietist groups arose in Europe during the sixteenth and seventeenth centuries because they believed that many who protested the errors of Catholicism had not gone far enough in their departures from Rome. Some of the Protestants were promoting a kind of *"cheap grace."* They were preaching forgiveness without repentance, baptism without discipline, and communion without loyalty to Bible standards.

The Anabaptists (who said infant baptism is invalid) and the Pietists (who insisted on godly Christian living) believed in *"costly grace"*—that is, they made so serious a commitment to Christ that they were determined to take the entire New Testament at face value. They aimed to put every command into practice, assuming that the text was interpreted in light of the original language and the accepted laws of interpretation. They tried to carefully obey *all* the Bible's teachings, not to gain favor with God, but to please the Lord who had first loved them. To the Anabaptists and Pietists, godly living was the outgrowth of the salvation which came to them through faith in Jesus Christ.

The intent of this commentary on the Bible book of Hebrews is to include a verse-by-verse series of comments and explanations that cover each verse of the thirteen chapters of the letter. Too many Christians know only the "heroes of faith" account in chapter 11 and a few other familiar texts (like 4:16, 9:22b, and 13:8), without understanding the total theme of this book. It is my hope that lay members of the church will use the commentary as a daily study guide, and that preachers and teachers of the Bible message will try to teach through the entire book of Hebrews in an expository series of sermons. The preparation of practical expository messages requires much careful study.

My primary goal has been to help lay members, and also Sunday school teachers and preachers who proclaim the Word of God to others, through an exposition and application of the Bible message. A special word of thanks goes to my wife, Priscilla, and to Martha Hess, for their help in proof-reading the manuscript for this commentary.

It is intended that the expositions and applications of the Bible text found *in this study tool* will be a blessing to Christian workers, young people in the church, parents in the home, and all who set out to study the New Testament Scriptures. Hopefully each group will share its findings with others. I suggest that readers keep an open Bible, so that it will be convenient to turn quickly to a variety of references, while using the pages of this commentary.

To *study* the Bible is our highest privilege. To *obey* it is our greatest responsibility. To *share* its message with others is to participate in bringing lasting joy to many hungry hearts. Those who teach Bible classes and those who preach the Word may feel free to use any part of these studies in any way they find helpful. May God use this book to steer believers from error and to bring souls to the Savior.

March 1, 2008
Harold S. Martin
26 United Zion Circle
Lititz, PA 17543

TABLE OF CONTENTS
The Book of Hebrews

9

INTRODUCTION TO HEBREWS

The nineteenth book of the New Testament is called the book of Hebrews. It begins with a magnificent tribute to Jesus Christ (1:1-3), and throughout the book there are warnings which are intended to encourage readers to hold fast to Jesus as God's great High Priest. Jesus is the only Mediator between God and man (1 Timothy 2:5).

The writer of the letter known as the book of Hebrews cannot be known with certainty.[1] It is our conviction that if God meant for us to know the writer's name,[2] He would have told us. As Origen, an early church leader said it: "Who wrote the epistle, to be sure, only God knows."

In the early New Testament church, unconverted Jews (Jews who were not Christians) used many arguments to try and draw their converted (Christian) Jewish friends away from the faith. They argued that the Law of Moses is superior to the Christian faith. The writer of Hebrews wanted the Jewish believers to see that they gained more in Christ than they had renounced in Judaism. (Judaism is the Jewish religion, based on the laws and teachings of the Old Testament and the Talmud.)

The key word in the book of Hebrews is "better," meaning more excellent, more desirable, and more suitable.

---

[1] The *King James Version* of the Bible speaks of this letter as "The Epistle of Paul the Apostle to the Hebrews"—but that title is not part of the inspired text. The Bible does not name the author, and it is not possible for us to do that with any degree of accuracy. It was Clement of Alexandria who suggested that Paul wrote the epistle. In certain places the letter's language is like Paul's. The closing verses are characteristic of Paul, for example 13:18, 19, and 25.

[2] Some of the names suggested as possible writers are Barnabas and Apollos. Barnabas was a Levite (Acts 4:36), and the epistle contains much that would be of special interest to a Levite, but the writer says that the message of salvation "was confirmed to us by those who heard Him" (2:3). Barnabas would hardly have written those words since he himself most likely heard Jesus.

The purpose for the book of Hebrews is to assure Jewish Christians that Old Testament Judaism has come to an end now that Christ has fulfilled the whole purpose of the Law. It was also designed to warn those who had identified themselves as Christians, against falling back into Judaism and abandoning true faith in Christ. A third purpose was to bring to the attention of Christians everywhere the superiority of the Lord Jesus Christ.[3]

We can likely understand Hebrews best if we remember that God has chosen to deal with the fallen human family in two broad periods of time—by working out two great covenants—the Old Covenant and the New Covenant (or, the Old Testament and the New Testament).

The Old Covenant served a good purpose, but it was *incomplete* without the death of Christ. Again, the Apostle Paul declares that Christ's death brought an end to the Mosaic Law. "Therefore the law was our tutor [schoolmaster] to bring us to Christ, that we might be justified by faith. But after faith has come, we are no longer under a tutor" (Galatians 3:24-25). The Old Testament Law (which has been done away) was glorious for its time and purpose, but that glory has faded behind the brilliant light of the grace of Christ. The Apostle Paul contrasts the New Covenant with the Old Covenant in this way: "For if what is passing away was glorious, what remains [or that which replaces it], is much more glorious" (2 Corinthians 3:11).

As a general rule of life, for God's people today, the

---

[3]   Robert Gromacki lists a number of purposes for the Hebrew letter. He says that the main purposes include these—to demonstrate the superiority of the person and work of Christ (1:1—10:18); to provoke readers to growth in Christian maturity (5:11-14); to comfort them in their persecutions (11:1—12:13); to warn them about the severity of divine chastisement (12:3-13); to alert them to the dangers of false teaching (13:9); and to request prayer for himself (13:18-25). The summary is found in *Stand Bold in Grace: Hebrews*, pages 16-17.

Mosaic Code has been replaced by what Paul calls in 1 Corinthians 9:21 "the law toward Christ." Some of the specific commands of the Old Code (for example, the Ten Commandments) are re-incorporated as requirements of the New Code, yet the Code itself has been "done away" (replaced). The Christians who had a Jewish background (Hebrew Christians) found it hard to give up the ceremonies and the teachings of Judaism. Judaism is a religion based on keeping precisely the 613 commandments of the Old Testament. The letter to the Hebrews emphasizes the supremacy of Christ—especially as contrasted with Judaism. A very general outline of the book follows.

There are three major sections. They are *The Superior Person of Christ* (1:1—7:28); *The Superior Provisions of Calvary* (8:1—10:18), and *The Superior Principles of Conduct* (10:19—13:25).

The letter begins by showing that Jesus is the Son of God, and therefore, He is superior to the angels and to the Old Testament prophets. The key verse is Hebrews 3:1, which says, *"Therefore, holy brethren, partakers of the heavenly calling, consider the Apostle and High Priest of our confession, Christ Jesus."*

The book of Hebrews describes in detail how Jesus Christ fulfills the promises and prophecies of the Old Testament. The Jews believed in the Old Testament, but most Jews rejected Jesus as the long awaited Messiah. Those who received this letter were likely well-versed in Scripture, and they had professed faith in Christ. They were in danger of giving up their faith and returning to Judaism—perhaps because of doubt, or persecution, or some false teaching which had influenced them.

One core concept in the book of Hebrews is the teaching that Jesus Christ is the only Mediator between God and man.

Only Jesus is the Author of our salvation. The book of Hebrews also emphasizes Christ's present priestly ministry of intercession at the right hand of God. In addition, there is the *Faith Hall of Fame*—a listing of Old Testament personalities who are cited as examples of men and women who believed God rewards those who seek Him.

The letter of Hebrews was probably written between 65 A.D. and 70 A.D. The date *before* 70 A.D. is generally given because it was in the year (70 A.D.) that Jerusalem (and the temple in the city) was destroyed by the Roman general Titus. Yet the book of Hebrews implies that the temple was still standing when the epistle was written (note Hebrews 8:4-5 and 10:11). There is, however, a hint in Hebrews 12:27 that the temple services might soon be removed.

The Jewish Temple was still standing when Hebrews was written, and the elaborate system of animal sacrifices was still in operation. Hebrews 10:11 implies that the priests were still actively participating in performing their duties at the time of the writing of Hebrews. All this had been beckoning Christians (who were formerly Jews) to forsake Christ and come back into the fold of Judaism. Jewish ties of family and friendship are very deep.

There are many strong warnings in the letter which indicate that the Hebrew Christians were in danger of forsaking Christ for their former religious practices in Judaism. The writer of Hebrews encourages the *Christians* to go on with Christ. It will be worth it all in the end.

Part I
THE SUPERIOR PERSON OF CHRIST
(Hebrews 1:1—7:28)

Chapter 1

CHRIST IS SUPERIOR TO THE PROPHETS
Hebrews 1:1-3

The book of Hebrews presents a series of word pictures that exalt Jesus Christ in His deity and His humanity, lifting up His sacrificial work on the cross, His priestly office, and His kingly glory.

One major purpose of the book is to discourage readers from turning away from Christ and going back into Judaism. Even today, Christians sometimes compare other world religions favorably with the Christian message and are tempted to turn away from simple faith in Christ.

The writer of Hebrews does not begin with the usual greetings and salutations that are typical of the other New Testament letters. The opening verses of Hebrews contain several great theological themes—revelation, incarnation, theism, creation, providence, deity, redemption, and ascension. Those themes are stated in a brief but grand statement in verses 1-3 of the first chapter of the book.

1. God's Revelation by the Prophets (1:1)

This letter, although likely written originally to a specific congregation, was intended for the entire church down through the years. Two important theological statements are found in verse 1, and four additional theological statements are found in verses 2 and 3.

(1:1) God, who at various times and in various ways spoke in time past to the fathers by the prophets,

The letter opens with the assumption that the living God exists. The first word is "God." He is alive and real.

a. Theism (1:1a)

When Christians speak of *God*, they refer to the one true God,[4] Who is the Creator and the Sustainer of the universe. God has spoken and we are to listen. There are a number of human responses to a study of the concept of God.

The *atheist* says there is no God.

The *agnostic* says he can't tell if there is a God.

The *materialist* boasts that he doesn't need God.

The *pagan* sometimes argues that *everything* is god.

The *Christian* answers that he can't get along without God.

What one believes about God affects his decisions and actions in life. Moses chose not to be called the son of Pharaoh's daughter (the grandson of the king of Egypt), but instead, to suffer ill-treatment with the people of God, because he saw "Him who is invisible" (Hebrews 11:27b).

b. Revelation (1:1b)

God *spoke*. He "spoke" at different times and in various ways "to the fathers by the prophets." That is, God *revealed* Himself to the human family—thus the word *revelation*.

The theological term *revelation* refers to God's disclosure of truth about Himself, which mankind could not otherwise know. God has *revealed* truth about man, sin, and salvation. In earlier times, God had communicated with man by the prophets, through visions and dreams—and now ultimately through Christ and the Bible.

Other religions are man's thoughts about God; Christi-

---

[4]   God has revealed Himself and His character by the use of about 300 names in the Bible. In Psalm 91:1-2, the Holy Spirit mentions four names for the true God almost in one breath. The "Most High" is the Hebrew *Elyon*—the One who owns everything. The "Almighty" is the Hebrew *El Shaddai*—the God who supplies our needs. The "Lord" is the Hebrew *Jehovah*—the eternal, unchangeable One. "My God" is the Hebrew *Elohim*—the Creator God who is in absolute control. For a more complete description of the basic names for God, see the book, "Names of God" written by Nathan Stone.

anity is a *revealed* religion. It is not based on man's thoughts about God, but on *God's revelation* (God's *revealing* Himself to mankind).

There are two basic categories of revelation—*general* revelation and *special* revelation.

God's *general* revelation is seen in His creation. The realm of nature, with its sights and smells and sounds—is filled with hints and clues about the presence and power of God. The lightning's flash, the spider's web, the galaxy's order, these are all impressions and whispers that tell something about the God who made them all. Psalm 19:1 says, "The heavens declare the glory of God; and the firmament shows His handiwork."[5]

Romans 1:20 says that since the creation of the world, God's invisible qualities (His eternal power and His divine nature) have been clearly seen. Martin Luther says in his commentary on Galatians, that all people have a general knowledge of God—but what God thinks of us, and what He wants to do for us, is not known apart from His *special* revelation found in the Bible.

Nature reveals much about God, but nature lacks any specific statements about God; something more is needed, and that is the purpose of God's *special* revelation. God has chosen to speak to mankind not only through creation, but through a special stream of human history which is recorded in the Bible. This is called "special revelation" because it carries a special message from God to the people of Israel, and to their spiritual heirs in the Christian church.

God *spoke directly* to Adam (Genesis 3:9), to Noah (Genesis 6:13), and to Jesus at His baptism (Matthew 3:17). At Mount Sinai, God spoke in such a way to Moses that the

---

[5]   The NIV translation says, "The *skies* proclaim the work of his hands."

people also could hear His voice (Exodus 19:9).[6] When God called Samuel, the Lord's voice was so similar to a human voice that Samuel thought it was the voice of Eli. God used actual words that issued in real sounds (1 Samuel 3:1-18).

God also spoke *through theophanies*, meaning that God sometimes appeared on earth in human form. He appeared to Abraham in Genesis 18:1. God spoke *through angels*, declaring that Jesus was "Immanuel...God with us" (Matthew 1:23). God spoke *through the prophets* (Hebrews 1:1),[7] and God speaks *through the New Testament* (1 John 5:9).[8]

When visitors are guided through underground caves in the United States, it is a common practice for the guide to have all the lights in the cavern turned off. The tourists are left in darkness so oppressive that they can almost *feel* it. Their eyes seem to have no use—and then, when suddenly the lights come back on, they pass out of the world of black darkness to a scene of unusual beauty. Life without God is like life in the absolute darkness of an underground cavern. Life is without meaning apart from God's revelation. *Revelation* is God turning on the light.

Ever since the world began, God had been speaking to mankind at different times and in various ways. He communicated directly with Adam and some others, but at times

---

[6]   "And the Lord said to Moses, 'Behold I come to you in the thick cloud, that the people may hear when I speak with you, and believe you forever.'"

[7]   Simon Kistemaker says, "Through the prophets from Moses to Malachi, God's revelation was recorded in written form as history, psalm, proverb, and prophecy. The prophets were all those saints called by God and filled with his Spirit to speak the Word as a progressive revelation that intimates the coming of Christ. In his first epistle, Peter speaks of them...in 1 Peter 1:10-12" (*New Testament Commentary: Hebrews*, page 26).

[8]   In 1 John 5:9 we read about "the witness of God which He has testified of His Son." In verse 10, John speaks of those who "believe the testimony that God has given of His Son." What is the testimony that "God has given about his Son" (NIV)? That testimony is the entire New Testament.

he spoke through prophets. Zacharias the priest acknowledged that the God of Israel "spoke by the mouth of His holy prophets" (Luke 1:70).

In Old Testament times, God had given only a *partial* revelation of Himself. He spoke through the prophets and angels, but it is in His Son (Jesus Christ) that He gives a *complete* revelation of Himself in these last days.

2. God's Revelation by His Son (1:2-3)

One of the major purposes of the book of Hebrews is to bring to the attention of Christians everywhere the preeminence (the superiority) of Jesus Christ.

(1:2) has in these last days spoken to us by His Son, whom He has appointed heir of all things, through whom also He made the worlds;

God's revelation through the prophets was truth, but it was not full and final truth. Jesus Christ is God's full and final word to mankind. Christ is much greater than the prophets, and in the New Testament Jesus speaks.

a. Incarnation (1:2a)

God has in these last days "spoken to us *by His Son*" (verse 2). In times past, God spoke in various ways, through laws, ceremonies, visions, kings, priests, judges, and prophets. But Christ is superior to the prophets. Jesus is God in human form; the prophets were mere men.

When Jesus was born of Mary, that conception and birth was not the beginning of a new person. Rather, by a miracle of the Holy Spirit, Jesus was conceived in the womb of the Virgin Mary as described in Luke 1:26-38. In some miraculous way, the Holy Spirit ushered the life of the eternal Christ into the body of Mary, and from her womb was born a Person who is the true expression of God—the Lord Jesus

Christ—the eternal Christ in human form.[9]

No one has ever seen *God* in His true essence, but His only begotten Son (Jesus Christ) has declared God (John 1:18). If humans want to see God, they must look to Jesus Christ. He is God's full and final word to man.

Later it will be noted that Christ was the Creator and *in Him* all things hold together. Christ is much greater than the prophets—and in the New Testament, readers hear *Christ* speak, not mere human prophets.

The phrase "these last days" (verse 2a) speaks of the entire present dispensation of grace. In the present New Testament age, God is speaking to us by His Son.

b. Creation and providence (1:2b, 3a)

Jesus has been "appointed heir of all things, through whom also He made the worlds." God created all things by His Son. These words remind the reader of Psalm 2, where God places the Messiah on the throne, and grants Him *the earth and its people* for His inheritance (Psalm 2:6-9), although He has not yet fully possessed the inheritance.[10]

Jesus Christ is the One who "made the worlds" (verse 2b). This includes not only the material created world, but the great ages (time-periods) of history as well. Creation, in the Bible, is attributed to the Father, the Son, and the Holy Spirit. Not only has Christ created the worlds, but He also is

---

[9]   Millard Erickson says that *the incarnation* "was the means by which the revelation of deity was conveyed. Scripture specifically states that God has spoken through or in his Son" (*Christian Theology*, page 190).

[10]   Since Jesus is the Son of God, He will become the heir of all that God possesses. Everything that exists will come under the final control of Jesus Christ. The Psalmist had already predicted that Jesus would one day be the heir of all that God possesses (Psalm 2:6-9). When Christ came to earth the first time, He became poor that we might be made rich (2 Corinthians 8:9). When He comes the second time, He will inherit all things, and those who have trusted Him will become "joint heirs" with Him (Romans 8:17).

"upholding all things by the word of His power" (verse 3a). The Lord Jesus is not some super-human creature (like the Greek god *Atlas*) who supposedly held up the world. Jesus had part in creation, and He also holds together all that He created. He commands the winds and the waves. He has power over disease and death. It is *His* power that keeps the planets in their places, and provides sustenance for all created things on the earth.[11]

(1:3) who being the brightness of His glory and the express image of His person, and upholding all things by the word of His power, when He had by Himself purged our sins, sat down at the right hand of the Majesty on high,

It is one of our Lord's functions to sustain the universe and its operation (Colossians 1:17). The word "upholding" is the translation of the Greek word *"pheron,"* which includes the concept of "moving toward some goal." We will be blessed by remembering *that He who is the Lord of the stars and planets*, is Lord of the circumstances in our lives!

c. Deity and effulgence (1:3a)

Jesus is "the brightness of [God's] glory, and the express image of His person."[12] Jesus is the exact representation of God's essence. This cannot mean physical likeness to God because God is a spirit, but Jesus perfectly represents the heavenly Father. He bears the very stamp of God's nature

---

[11]   Psalm 104:25 lifts up the glory of God by mentioning the "great and wide sea in which are innumerable…living things both small and great." One blue whale, for example, is longer than three dump trucks, heavier than 100 mid-sized automobiles, and has a heart the size of a Volkswagen Beetle. Each whale consumes about four tons of food each day. Even a baby blue whale drinks about 100 gallons of milk every 24 hours. When we think of the countless living things in the sea, the vast hordes of land animals, and the more than six billion people on earth—the Lord Jesus performs a stupendous task in providing food for all living things.

[12]   The word translated "brightness" is *apaugasma*, and is rendered "the radiance of God's glory" in the NIV translation of the New Testament.

and reflects the glory of God. Just as Moses reflected the glory of God in the brightness of his countenance (after being in the presence of God for 40 days on Sinai), so Christ perfectly reflected the glory of the Father in that He was always in the fellowship of the Father.

Jesus is the disclosure of God's visible form. We do not see *in the incarnate Son*, the full expression of the *absolute* attributes of God—His immensity, immutability, and infinity—but in Jesus Christ we see the exact expression of God's personality and God's glory.

d. Redemption and ascension (1:3b)

Jesus had by Himself purged our sins. No mention of Jesus would be complete without mentioning His work for us when He died on the cross as our Substitute. When Jesus suffered on the cross He was making a perfect offering for our eternal salvation. Only *God* can purge our sins.

Jesus is the One who ascended into Heaven and is now *seated* at the right hand of God.[13] Following His redemptive work on the cross, He was given a place of honor (far beyond that of any prophet) by being exalted at the right hand of the heavenly Father. It was a place of special favor.[14]

The first three verses of Hebrews give God's portrait of Jesus Christ. They portray Him as a prophet (a spokesman for God); a priest (one who atones and intercedes); and a king (one who controls, sustains, and is seated on a throne). Surely, Jesus far surpasses others who have been considered some of the world's great saviors and teachers—Confucius, Buddha, and Muhammad.

---

[13] Jesus (by His death and resurrection) settled the sin question forever, and then ascended into Heaven, and sat down at the right hand of God. His work of redemption was completed.

[14] Homer A. Kent says that often "in our society, we speak of someone's 'right hand man'" (*The Epistle to the Hebrews*, page38).

Chapter 2

CHRIST IS SUPERIOR TO THE ANGELS
Hebrews 1:4—2:18

Christ is superior to the angels; this can be seen in that the angels actually *worship* Christ (1:6). Although angels are great in power and position, still they are subject to Jesus Christ, and worship the living God. No angel has ever been called the Son of God. The *greatness of Christ* is pointed out in this section of Hebrews in several ways.

1. Christ is Superior Because of His Deity (1:4-14)

Jesus Christ is God the Son. He is not a mere creature like the angels are. Angels are created beings; Christ is much greater because He is one with the Father.

a. He is the Son of God (1:4-5)

(1:4-5) having become so much better than the angels, as He has by inheritance obtained a more excellent name than they. For to which of the angels did He ever say: "You are My Son, Today I have begotten You"? And again: "I will be to Him a Father, and He shall be to Me a Son"?

We saw the superiority of Jesus to the prophets in that He was seated "at the right hand of the Majesty on high" (verse 3b). Now we see that the "name"[15] of Jesus marks Him as superior to the angels (verse 4a).

Angels are *messengers*; Jesus is *the Son*. His *name* is far more excellent than that of any created angel. Angels are mere *servants* "sent forth to minister for those who will in-herit salvation" (Hebrews 1:14). By way of contrast, Jesus is

---

[15]   In New Testament times a "name" was more than a mere way of identifying a person. A *name* summed up all that the person was and stood for. Except for nicknames, our culture does not connect a child's personality with his name.

the Son, a "better" name[16] indicating superior qualities. Jesus Christ is "Son" in a way that no one else is.

In verses 4-5 (of Hebrews 1) there is a quote from the Old Testament, Psalm 2:7. The Psalm does not explicitly mention *Christ*, but the inspired writer of Hebrews obviously sees the Psalm as bearing witness to Christ.

b. He is the object of angel worship (1:6-7)

(1:6-7) But when He again brings the firstborn into the world, He says: "Let all the angels of God worship Him." And of the angels He says: "Who makes His angels spirits and His ministers a flame of fire."

In this section the writer of Hebrews calls attention to a number of Old Testament Scriptures to show the superiority of the Son to the angels. The quote here is from the Septuagint translation[17] of Deuteronomy 32:43. The point is that angels *worship* the Son, who is greater than they.

Verse 7 is a quote from Psalm 104:4. God's angels are spirits who are powerful like "a flame of fire." Still, the powerful angels *worship* Jesus the Son of God.

c. He is God (1:8-9)

(1:8-9) But to the Son He says: "Your throne, O God, is forever and ever; a scepter of righteousness is the scepter of Your Kingdom. You have loved righteousness and hated lawlessness; therefore God, Your God, has anointed You with the oil of gladness more than Your companions."

The term "forever and ever" (verse 8) conveys the idea of His eternity. The words of both verses emphasize the sovereignty and the *eternity* of the Son. His throne, His

---

[16] This is the first use of the word "better" in the book of Hebrews, a term that occurs many times in the epistle.

[17] The *Septuagint* is a translation of the Bible from Hebrew into Greek. It was translated by 70 Jewish scholars and is sometimes designated as the LXX. Its translators based some parts of the translation on a Hebrew text that differs from the main sources used today for the Hebrew Bible.

scepter,[18] His kingdom—all of these qualities surpass His "companions"—a reference to the angels who are being discussed in the passage.[19] The word "anointed" here carries the meaning of "being authorized or set apart for a particular work or service." The Messiah was "the Anointed One."

The words of verses 8-9 are quoted from Psalm 45:6-7, and the heavenly Father addresses His Son *as God*.[20] Keep in mind that just because He is called "My Son" (verse 5) does not mean that He is less than God. It is true that "*the son of the President" is not* the President of the United States, but in Jewish tradition the phrase *son of* did not imply subordination; rather, it implied equality and identity of nature.[21]

d. He is Jehovah (1:10-13)

(1:10-13) And: "You, LORD, in the beginning laid the foundation of the earth, and the heavens are the work of Your hands. They will perish, but You remain; and they will all grow old like a garment; like a cloak You will fold them up, and they will be changed. But You are the same, and Your years will not fail." But to which of the angels has He ever said: "Sit at My right hand, till I make Your enemies Your footstool"?

---

[18] The "scepter" refers to "the official staff of a ruler, symbolizing his authority and…sometimes the symbolism of a scepter refers to the Messiah who will rule from Israel…the book of Hebrews describes Christ as the Son who rules with a scepter of righteousness" (*Nelson's Illustrated Bible Dictionary*, page 956).

[19] John MacArthur says, "The point being made here is that Jesus Christ is greater than angels, who are His associates, His heavenly companions" (MacArthur *New Testament Commentary on Hebrews*, page 28).

[20] Our Anabaptist forefathers held clearly to the teaching that Jesus Christ is God the Son. Mennonite writer, Daniel Kauffman, devotes an entire chapter to this teaching in his book on Bible doctrines. The Scripture he uses to introduce the chapter is Hebrews 1:8 (See *Doctrines of the Bible*, pages 61-69).

[21] For example, Barnabas was called "Son of Encouragement" because he was an encourager (Acts 4:36). James and John were called "Sons of Thunder" because they were thunderous men (Mark 3:17). When Jesus said, "I am the Son of God" (John 10:36), He claimed equality and identity with God.

These verses are taken from Psalm 102:25-27, and in that Psalm the Father is addressed as "LORD" (the word is *Jehovah* in Hebrew). Jehovah is one of the most important names for God in the Old Testament. The word means "to be," a profound name which actually declares "I am who I am" and "I will be who I will be." When God spoke to Moses from the burning bush, Moses was told to say, *"I AM has sent me to you"* (Exodus 3:14). Jesus also is the *I AM* (John 8:58), and thus He described Himself as One who possessed absolute eternal existence.

The quote in verse 13 is taken from Psalm 110:1. This Psalm is often referred to in the New Testament, and it is always applied to Christ Jesus. In fact Jesus Himself said that the Psalm refers to Him (Mark 12:35-37).

Jesus is not only *God* (verse 8), and *Jehovah* (verse 10); He is also *Adonai* (the LORD in verse 13; see Psalm 110:1 for the complete quote), meaning that He is the Sovereign or Ruler.

e. Angels are ministering spirits (1:14)

(1:14) Are they not all ministering spirits sent forth to minister for those who will inherit salvation?

Jesus is the eternal God. The angels, by way of contrast, are mere *servants*. They have been "sent forth" to minister for those who have salvation.

Angels are heavenly beings that are superior to man in power and intelligence. They are *spirit* beings[22] that have superhuman power (2 Peter 2:11) and wisdom (2 Samuel 14:17,20). Angels, however, are not *all* powerful and *all* knowing beings (Mark 13:32; 1 Peter 1:12).

---

[22] Even though we may never have seen an angel, or heard one speak, nevertheless they exist and exert their influence all the same. For a more exhaustive study of *angels* as described in the Bible, see the small (97 pages) but useful book entitled, *The Ministry of Angels*, written by A. S. Joppie. Another helpful study is entitled, *Angels, God's Secret Agents*, written by Billy Graham.

A *TIME* magazine poll[23] indicates that most Americans believe in angels, although *students of the Bible* sense that many hold wrong concepts about angels. Much misinformation is related to distorted pictures, varied superstitions, and ignorance of Bible facts. We are not to *worship* angels. They are not gods, but merely God's servants—but they are real and they minister in behalf of God's people.

Examples of angel ministry in New Testament times are found in many places. Matthew 28:2 mentions that an angel rolled the heavy stone away from the entrance to the tomb where Jesus was buried. Acts 12:7 tells that an angel was used of God to deliver Peter from prison. In Luke 16:22, Jesus says that angels carried the poor man to the bosom of Abraham at the time of his death. There have been some striking accounts of angel ministry in our day.[24]

The major point of Hebrews 1:5-14 is that Christ is far superior to the angels.[25] He is greater than angels, for His name is *God the Son*; the angels actually worship Him (1:6),

---

[23]   The article in *TIME* magazine is entitled "Angels Among Us" and appeared in the December 27, 1993 issue of *TIME*. The poll says that 69% of Americans believe in angels, and 46% believe that people have a personal guardian angel.

[24]   Marie Monsen was a Norwegian missionary serving in North China. She gave testimony about the intervention of angels at times when Christians were in danger. "On one occasion, when looting soldiers surrounded her mission compound, those who had taken refuge within its flimsy walls were astonished to find that they were left in peace. A few days later, the marauders [themselves] explained that they were ready to enter, when they noticed tall soldiers with shining faces on a high roof in the compound. And a [nearby] unbeliever said…'there were many people standing on the east verandah all last night; who were they?' Marie Monsen said, 'The heathen saw the [tall soldiers]; it was a testimony to them, but they were invisible to us'" (*Christ above All: The Message of Hebrews, BST series*, Raymond Brown, pages 45-46).

[25]   Brethren writer, R. H. Miller, in his 1876 volume entitled *The Doctrine of the Brethren Defended*, says that Jesus "laid the foundation of the earth and built the heavens, and that when they shall all perish, He will still remain" (page 23). The Brethren did not detour around the plain Bible truths, even when reading those accounts that had to be accepted by simple faith.

and He is the One who created and sustains the earth. Jesus Christ is not a mere creature like angels are. The angels are created beings. Christ is Creator and the One who upholds all things. He laid the foundations of the earth (1:10), and is now seated at the right hand of God (1:13).

2. *First warning passage—danger of neglect (2:1-4)*

Throughout the book of Hebrews there are warning passages in which sin is denounced, especially the sins of unbelief and disobedience.

(2:1) Therefore we must give the more earnest heed to the things we have heard, lest we drift away.

The first warning passage[26] [in 2:1-4] points out the danger of neglect. The "things we have heard" were the teachings of Christ and those gospel truths which have been previously taught by the Lord's apostles.

We are called to give "more earnest heed to the things we have heard" (verse 1),[27] which means that it is imperative for us to pay attention to the gospel message.[28] If Christ is all that the writer of the first chapter of Hebrews says He

---

[26] There will be additional warning passages throughout the book of Hebrews. There are three views concerning the warning sections: (1) They speak only of *professing* Christians, that is, people who professed faith in Christ, but were never really saved; these words then are warning them not to stop short of getting saved. (2) They speak of *real believers, but* of those who are in danger of becoming barren and without fruit, and thus in danger of losing a reward. (3) They speak of *true Christians* who could eventually lose salvation by failing to maintain an on-going faith in Christ. This commentary writer believes that the third option is the proper interpretation.

[27] Richard Taylor says, "We might be careless about listening to the chatter of a neighbor, but we would pay the most rapt attention to the head of state" (*Beacon Bible Commentary,* Volume 10, page 32).

[28] The word "must" [translated "ought" in KJV] (verse 1a) is a strong word which removes any doubt about whether or not the command should be performed. There are no other options. We *must* give heed to what we have heard. The same word is used in Luke 2:49, John 9:4, Luke 9:22, etc.

is—then it is essential for us to hold on to those things that He has taught, and let those truths make a difference in our thinking and in our everyday lives.

Unless we devote ourselves to embracing the Christian truths that we have been taught, we can "drift away" from faithfulness to the gospel. The drifting usually comes upon individuals gradually. At first there is no dramatic sense of departure, but when the storms of trouble come, they discover that their faith is not anchored very deeply.

(2:2) For if the word spoken through angels proved steadfast, and every transgression and disobedience received a just reward,

The "word spoken through angels" (verse 2) refers to *the law* given at Sinai. The Old Testament account of giving the law does not mention angels, but in the New Testament, Stephen declared that the law was received by the direction of angels (Acts 7:53), and the Apostle Paul said that the law was mediated by angels (Galatians 3:19).

Disobedience to the law in Old Testament days brought swift judgment. The writer of Hebrews does not list specific examples of punishment—but Bible students remember that if persons committed adultery, worshiped false gods, or blasphemed God, they were stoned. Punishing violations of the law was sure and certain.[29] Verse 2b says that "every transgression and disobedience received a just reward."[30]

We need to remember the defiance of Nadab and Abihu, and the swift punishment that came by means of a devouring fire (Leviticus 10:1-5). Every transgression (stepping across the line) and disobedience (failing to comply with commands) received a quick and fair punishment.

---

[29]   See Deuteronomy 22:22-24; 13:1-10; 17:2-7; and Leviticus 20:27.
[30]   The "just reward" (Greek, *endikon misthapodosian*) refers to "a payment of wages; punishment" (*Thayer's Greek Lexicon*, page 415).

(2:3) how shall we escape if we neglect so great a salvation, which at the first began to be spoken by the Lord, and was confirmed to us by those who heard Him,

If the message of the Old Testament could not be violated without suffering severe consequences, how much more should we treasure the message of salvation by grace as revealed in the New Testament? Should not *more respect* be given to the message that came not through angels, but through the Son? If we neglect the message of redemption through Jesus Christ, it will be impossible for us to escape God's wrath and His punishment.

The word "neglect" (Greek, *amelesamtes*) means "to fail to care for" or "to fail to give proper attention to." It is easy for Christians *to neglect* this great salvation because it is largely invisible and spiritual. One of the cardinal sins of Christians is to neglect *private devotions*—taking time *daily* for prayer and careful reading of the Word of God. From such neglect, stem many other sins that bring much dishonor and reproach to the name of Christ.

Those who neglect their salvation will soon find that *their defenses are lowered.* Human beings are capable of doing the very highest acts of kindness in one moment, and the very next moment they can be cruel and unkind. At one moment humans seem to have a little spark of God, and the next time they seem to be under the influence of the devil himself. This is true for the new believer, as well as for the saint of ripe years. There is no sin that any person can be quite sure he will never commit.

Neglecting salvation is often the result of *giving in* to the luring influences of the world around us, the tendency of the carnal mind to focus on *this life* instead of the life to come, and the inclination to ignore the means of grace, including the regular assembly with God's people. *Now*, there are many opportunities to feed on the message of the Bible, and in this way grow strong spiritually. For many, it will not always be so. We are living in a time of grace, but the time may very well come when believers will be scattered and exposed to persecution. Those who are careless now will undoubtedly fail in the time of difficult trial.

We must never underestimate the value of salvation. It was attained for us at the price of the suffering and death of Jesus. Our salvation is "so great" because it was planned by God and offered through the blood atonement of His Son, and is available to us on the basis of the undeserved, un-merited and unearned grace of God (Ephesians 2:8-10). Do not neglect it.

(2:4) God also bearing witness both with signs and won-ders, with various miracles, and gifts of the Holy Spirit, ac-cording to His own will?

The thought of verse 3b is continued in verse 4. God bore witness to the truthfulness of the salvation message by confirming what the early apostles proclaimed, with signs and wonders and various miracles,[31] and with gifts of the Holy Spirit.[32] The New Testament gospel message is con-firmed and reliable. It is not speculation; it is a revelation from God, through Jesus Christ, and affirmed by His apos-tles. The gospel of Jesus Christ is God's truth; it is not a compilation of man's ideas.

The salvation that the writer mentions (in 2:1-4) is the

---

[31]   The phrase "signs and wonders" occurs twelve times in the New Testament, most often in the first fifteen chapters of Acts. The word "miracles" is used to describe the supernatural deeds of Jesus, and is recorded mostly in the first three Gospels. Peter used all three terms (signs, wonders, miracles) in his sermon on Pentecost (Acts 2:22). The three terms emphasize the supernatural power asso-ciated with the mighty works of God.

[32]   The "gifts of the Holy Spirit" refer to those special abilities given to believers by the Holy Spirit (1 Corinthians 12:4-11).

salvation that God revealed in this present age through the Lord Jesus, and was confirmed to us by those who heard Him. God Himself joined in the witness to the veracity of the Good News of salvation through faith in the work of His Son Jesus Christ. The message of salvation, and its implications for the Christian life, is to be heeded. To fail to pay attention to God's gift of salvation holds the threat of judgment.

3. Christ is Superior Because of His Humanity (2:5-18)

It was man who sinned and it is man who needs to pay for sin. Jesus at His incarnation took on humanity, and in that sense is superior to the angels who have never adopted human characteristics.[33]

a. Christ's love for humanity (2:5-9)

Everything that God has done from the beginning of creation has been planned for the delight of mankind. He desired man to have dominion over the created world. The world was a beautiful place, and man was created to have authority over it. "But now we do not yet see all things put under him" (verse 8b). Sin entered the human race, and now, instead of being a king, man became a slave.

(2:5-9) For He has not put the world to come, of which we speak, in subjection to angels. But one testified in a certain place, saying: "What is man that You are mindful of him, Or the son of man that You take care of him? You have made him a little lower than the angels; You have crowned him with glory and honor, and set him over the works of Your hands. You have put all things in subjection under his feet." For in that He put all in subjection under him, He left nothing that is not put under him. But now we do not yet see all things put under him. But we see Jesus, who *[for a little while, marginal*

---

[33] Chapter 2:1-4 was a parenthesis in the flow of thought, which means that the reader should go from 1:14 directly to 2:5 to maintain the order of thinking.

note] **was made lower than the angels, for the suffering of death crowned with glory and honor, that He, by the grace of God, might taste death for everyone.**

The "world to come" (verse 5) speaks of a future age on this inhabited earth, and refers to that time when the kingdoms of this world become the kingdom of our Lord and His Christ (the millennial kingdom). Angels will not rule in that day.[34] In that kingdom of righteousness, human beings (who are *insignificant* and yet crowned with *dignity*, as noted in Psalm 8) will participate in the rule—but because of the fall into sin, their participation is limited.

In verses 6-8 there is a quote from the eighth Psalm. It is sometimes understood that there is *no difference* between the words "man" and "son of man" (verse 6).[35] On the other hand, the words seem to refer to Jesus, the Son of Man. The purpose of the text then is to show that during the time of His *humiliation*, Jesus was inferior to the angels, but during His *exaltation* He is far above them.

Only of Jesus can it be said that "all things" have been put in subjection under His feet (verse 8a).[36] Jesus Christ is appointed the Ruler over the whole earth, in order to deliver

---

[34] It was never God's purpose that angels should rule over humanity. God has used angels to be servants for His people here on earth. They appeared from time to time to announce blessings (as at the birth of Jesus in Luke 2) and to warn of judgment (as at the death of Herod Agrippa in Acts 12), but it is not in the plan of God to have angels administer government.

[35] The thought in 2:8 is not very clear. Is the writer thinking of Christ or man in this verse? The marginal note (in NKJV study Bibles) indicates that the phrase "a little lower than the angels" could be translated "for a little while lower than the angels" in both verse 7 and verse 9. If *that reading* is more accurate, the reference from Psalm 8 *in Hebrews 2*, most likely refers *to Jesus* as "the Son of man."

[36] The *Living Bible* paraphrase catches the essence of verses 6-8. *"What is mere man that you are so concerned about him? And who is this Son of Man you honor so highly? For though you made him lower than the angels for a little while, now you have crowned him with glory and honor. And you have put him in complete charge of everything there is."*

it from the bondage and corruption into which it has fallen. God has appointed Christ as heir of all things, and has decreed that all shall be in subjection under His feet (verse 8). Human beings are not what they ought to be, but Jesus is. He experienced every form of temptation and defeated it.

If Jesus is able to "taste death for everyone" (verse 9b), He must become Man, for only a man could pay for men's sins. And so Jesus was for a while made a little lower than the angels for a clear purpose—that is, for "the suffering of death...that He, by the grace of God, might taste death for everyone" (verse 9b). His great sacrifice on the cross was a clear mark of Christ's love for the human family.

Jesus *tasted* death for everyone. What does that mean? The word "taste" (Greek, *geusetai*) means to "actually experience death's bitterness." His *tasting death* was not a mere sip or sampling; it was an actual experience. The same word is used in Matthew 16:28 and John 8:52.

Christ's *love* for mankind is humanly impossible to explain. We are not lovable, but Christ *loved us* because He wanted us to be saved for eternity.

b. Christ's identification with humanity (2:10-14a)

Jesus did not take upon Himself the nature of angels. He bypassed those exalted beings and came down to us, taking on a flesh and blood body.

(2:10-14a) For it was fitting for Him, for whom are all things and by whom are all things, in bringing many sons to glory, to make the captain of their salvation perfect through sufferings. For both He who sanctifies and those who are being sanctified are all one, for which reason He is not ashamed to call them brethren, saying: "I will declare Your name to My brethren; In the midst of the assembly I will sing praise to You." And again: "I will put My trust in Him." And again: "Here am I and the children whom God has given

Me." Inasmuch then as the children have partaken of flesh and blood, He Himself likewise shared in the same,

Our Lord's task is to "bring many sons to glory" (verse 10), and so we read about Christ being made "perfect through sufferings" (verse 10b).

The words, "to make the captain of their salvation perfect through sufferings," do *not* refer to *the maturing* that the experience of suffering usually brings to individuals. Jesus always has been perfect in a moral sense. He is sinless. The reference here is to the fact that on the cross Jesus made *perfect* (that is, *complete*)[37] all the requirements that were necessary for the work of redemption.

The expression, "He who sanctifies, and those who are being sanctified, are all of one" (verse 11), means that Christ has become Man and thus shared the humanity of believers. Verse 14 repeats the truth. Union with Christ means that we are His brothers and sisters,[38] and He is not ashamed to call us that. In verses 12-13, the writer quotes Psalm 22:22 and Isaiah 8:17-18 in order to support the thought of verse 11.

Jesus Christ, who is God, partook of "flesh and blood" (verse 14a), and thus united His divine nature with human nature to become a "God-Man." The nature of the work which Jesus came to accomplish demanded that He take on human flesh and blood. It was man who had sinned; it is man

---

[37] The Greek term, *teleioo*, means "to carry to consummation" (or *to complete*), (*Hebrews in the Greek New Testament*, Kenneth S. Wuest, page 60).

[38] While there is a sense in which we are brothers of our Lord, yet in a sense His relationship with the Father differs from ours. "Jesus' relationship to the Father is so different from ours that He could say, 'You have only one Master and you are all brothers' (Matthew 23:8), excluding Himself from the group of brothers" (*Bible Study Commentary: Hebrews*, Leon Morris, page 32). Before the cross, Jesus called His followers—*disciples* or *friends* or *sheep*, but never *brothers*—yet as soon as He arose from the dead, He said to the women who had come early in the morning to see the tomb, "Go and tell My *brethren* to go to Galilee, and there they will see Me" (Matthew 28:10).

who needs to atone for sin. This was the primary reason why Jesus became Man and identified with humanity.

All mankind stands guilty before God because we have sinned. It is not necessary to blame Adam, for we would have made the same choice if we had been in his place. Adam plunged us into an attitude of rebellion against God, and mankind has never changed from that direction. God wants to bring us back. He wants to make us new persons. He wants to free us from the shackles of sin, so that we can look forward to a place where time and suffering and death are no longer present. He wants to give us eternity.

Christ partook of flesh and blood and assumed human nature. He did not take on the nature of angels, which are spirit beings and normally do not inhabit material bodies.

c. Christ's deliverance of humanity (2:14b-18)

Jesus delivered us from the fear of death. Death here refers not only to physical death but to spiritual death as well. It includes condemnation and eternal separation from God.

(2:14b-18) that through death He might destroy him who had the power of death, that is, the devil, and release those who through fear of death were all their lifetime subject to bondage. For indeed He does not give aid to angels, but He does give aid to the seed of Abraham. Therefore, in all things He had to be made like His brethren, that He might be a merciful and faithful High Priest in things pertaining to God, to make propitiation for the sins of the people. For in that He Himself has suffered, being tempted, He is able to aid those who are tempted.

In what sense was the devil *destroyed* through the death of Jesus (verse 14b)? The word "destroy" (Greek, *katargesei*) means *to render inoperative*, not *to annihilate*. Satan's power *was broken* as a result of Christ's death, but for the present, Satan is far from being destroyed in any *final* sense.

He lurks "like a roaring lion" seeking someone to terrorize (1 Peter 5:8)—but Christ's death robbed the devil of his earlier power, and ultimately he will be completely destroyed.

The "fear of death" (verse 15) is the effect of sin, and the awareness of God's displeasure with sin. The fear of what lies beyond death keeps many a person in the bondage of misery all his life. All human beings know that they are unworthy of a heavenly reward. The writer of Hebrews wanted to make sure that his readers understood that the power of Satan has been broken (nullified) by Christ. The cringing fear of death is a pitiful kind of bondage which shackles the entire human race. The bondage is broken by acknowledging that death has been conquered by Christ's own death and resurrection.[39]

While it is true that God alone controls the matter of life and death (Job 2:6; Luke 12:5), it is also true that it was the work of the devil that brought death into the world.[40] Adam's sin was brought about by the temptation put before him by

---

[39] Raymond Brown illustrates: "I used to be a postman. One day I had to deliver a letter to a house I had never visited before. I opened the garden gate only to find myself confronted by the largest and most vicious dog I had ever seen! It barked furiously and then leapt toward me. I stood there helpless and terrified until, to my immense relief, I saw that this massive, angry dog was chained to a huge stake set in concrete. The chain was a long one and the dog had considerable freedom, but not enough to reach me. I saw I could easily deliver the letter and I did so. That incident became like a parable to me. As a matter of fact, whenever I had to visit that house in the course of my work, I took little notice of the aggressive dog. I always kept my eye on the strong stake! [Just so, in a spiritual sense], at the cross, the enemy of our souls, the devil, was made impotent, limited and chained down. When he has 'bitten us' it is usually because we have been far too near" (see *Christ Above All: The Message of Hebrews*, BST series, by Raymond Brown, page 70).

[40] "Satan [is] not to be thought of as a mythological *symbol* of evil, but a *person* with power and authority in his own right." (Richard Taylor, *Beacon Bible Commentary: Hebrews*, page 38). Satan's kingdom of darkness was deeply involved in the chaos of man's fall into sin. Satan, in the form of a serpent, was present already in the Garden of Eden.

the devil (Genesis 3:1-19). Thus it is correct to say that the devil exercises power in the realm of death (2:14b).

Christ's death has brought defeat to the power of the devil, and that defeat has led to freedom from the enslavement to fear which had gripped multitudes of people. When an individual receives Christ as Savior, death holds no more fear.[41] We all have some uneasiness about that which we have never experienced before, but we actually look forward to death (Philippians 1:21). Death simply releases us into the presence of the Lord. The inscriptions on the tombs of *pagan people* are loaded with words of grief and hopelessness. By way of contrast, the tombs (catacombs) of the *early Christians* are marked with words of confidence and hope.

When Jesus "made propitiation for the sins of the people" (verse 17b), angels were not included (verse 16). Jesus made reconciliation between man and God (2 Corinthians 5:18-21). He was our Substitute. He stood in the place of sinners and paid the price that our sins demanded (Isaiah 53:4-6). The shedding of Jesus' blood on the cross was a once-for-all sacrifice which becomes effective for our salvation when claimed by faith.

Jesus was "tempted" (verse 18) in the same areas in which we are tempted. He faced the temptations that we experience, yet with no tendency to sin. Jesus came through victoriously, and thus is fitted to bear the sins of humanity, for He is both *essential Deity* and *perfect Manhood*.

In summary, Jesus died in our place (2:9), conquered our enemy the devil (2:14b), and secured our salvation (2:17b). Jesus Christ is the Son of God. Angels are mere creatures, and thus Jesus is much greater than the angels.

---

[41] An anonymous poem says, "Afraid of what? Afraid to pass from pain to perfect peace? Afraid to see the Savior's face? Afraid to hear His welcome?"

Chapter 3

CHRIST IS SUPERIOR TO MOSES AND AARON
Hebrews 3:1—4:13

It is obvious that the readers of Hebrews were Christians, but it seems that they were thinking less and less of Christ and more and more of their Old Testament heroes.

In Old Testament times, *Moses* was the man through whom the law had been given. *Aaron* was the first high priest in Israel. These were two great men, but they themselves were sinners, and so they had to offer animal sacrifices to atone for their own sins (Hebrews 5:1-3). It is not so with Christ. He had no sins (Hebrews 7:26-27).

1. Christ in His Work is Superior to Moses (3:1-4)

Believers are to consider Jesus, who is "the Apostle and High Priest" of our confession.

(3:1-2) Therefore, holy brethren, partakers of the heavenly calling, consider the Apostle and High Priest of our confession, Christ Jesus, who was faithful to Him who appointed Him, as Moses also was faithful in all His house.

The word *holy* (verse 1) means "set apart." Those who have turned to Christ for salvation are His *brethren*. The term "holy brethren" refers to *sanctification*—both in position and in experience.[42] From God's point of view, those who have embraced Christ as Savior are by faith set apart from the world, and are to be separate from the pagan world in their daily conduct. Believers are called "holy breth-

---

[42] There is a sanctification in *position,* a setting apart by Christ at the time of conversion (Hebrews 10:10; Acts 26:18). There is a sanctification in *experience* (Ephesians 5:26; John 17:17). And there will also be an *ultimate* sanctification (compare 1 John 3:2; Romans 8:29).

ren"—those, who by God's grace are declared holy, and are brought into a new family, the family of God.

Christians are "partakers of the heavenly calling" (3:1), a calling initiated by God as He seeks us out and calls us to come to Him (John 6:44). A "partaker" is someone who shares something together with someone else. The word describes partnership in some common blessing. That is why a doctor can sit next to a trash collector when God's people assemble together; they are brothers in the family of God and partakers of the same heavenly calling.

The call to *"consider...Christ Jesus"* is an appeal to have the partners in the heavenly calling think seriously and carefully about Jesus, who works as an "Apostle" and a "High Priest." Believers are to fix their attention continuously on the Lord Jesus. Christians with a Jewish background had a great heritage in men such as Moses, but the writer here wanted to show how much better Jesus is.

The word "Apostle" means "one who is sent on a mission." Jesus is God's ambassador to earth sent by the Father. Jesus had been sent to fulfill a definite mission for God. He not only came to provide the way of salvation (Mark 10:45), but also to establish a household (a redeemed community), as stated in Ephesians 2:18-22.

The term "High Priest" really means "bridge builder." A *priest* is the person who is set aside to serve as a mediator between the worshiper and his God. Jesus is the One who built the bridge to span the gulf between God and man.

(3:3-4) For this One has been counted worthy of more glory than Moses, inasmuch as He who built the house has more honor than the house. For every house is built by someone, but He who built all things is God.

One of the arguments of this section is that Christ is the eternal *Son* over the household; Moses is only a temporary *servant*. The word "house" used here does not refer to a building made with bricks, but to a household of people. The word "house"[43] was used to describe God's people.

One of the arguments in verses 3-4, is that Christ is better than Moses because Christ is *the builder* of God's house, while Moses was merely *a servant* in the household. Moses, as a man, is part of the household. There is one house, of which Jesus is the Builder, and over which, as Son, He rules. By way of contrast, Moses, as part of the building, is an honored[44] servant.

2. Christ in His Person is Superior to Moses (3:5-6)

Moses was faithful, but he was only a servant in God's household, while Christ is a Son and He is Master over His own household (verses 5-6).

(3:5-6) And Moses indeed was faithful in all His house as a servant, for a testimony of those things which would be spoken afterward, but Christ as a Son over His own house, whose house we are if we hold fast the confidence and the rejoicing of the hope firm to the end.

No one in the Old Testament was considered closer to God than was Moses (Exodus 33:7-11; 18-23)—but even he was only a servant in God's house, while Jesus is the Son.

Moses was "faithful in all His house"—that is, Moses did everything God required of him. Exodus 40:16 says that Moses "did...all that the Lord had commanded him"—but

---

[43] The Greek word *oikos* means "a household," a reference to the people of God—either the church of the New Testament or the people of Israel of the Old Testament times. The term "house" is a synonym for "the family of God."

[44] Moses is not in any way discredited by the argument, for he is said to have been a *faithful* servant (3:5) in the house, but Christ is the owner. God had honored Moses in many ways. He appeared to Moses face to face (Exodus 33:11); He gave him a long life of 120 years to live, and when Moses died, God buried him (Deuteronomy 34:6).

verse 6 shows that the greatness and glory of Jesus surpasses even the loyalty of Moses.

The clause "if we hold fast the confidence and the rejoicing of hope firm to the end" (verse 6b)—means that it is a serious matter *not to continue in the faith*. There is no casual, easy-going description of Christianity in the New Testament. The Bible never encourages complacency.

The warning in theses verses is similar to many others in the book of Hebrews. The fact that we are part of God's family is *conditional*. While salvation is by the grace of God, it is also true that the Lord expects His disciples to persevere in the faith.[45] Those who hold fast their confidence firmly to the end—are part of the house of God (are saved), and those who harden their hearts, by implication, will be lost.

3. *Second warning passage—danger of unbelief (3:7—4:13)*

When individuals are confronted by the call of God to devote their lives to Him—it is important that they respond to the Lord's call in faith.

a. *Danger of being hardened to God's voice (3:7-11)*

(3:7-11) Therefore, as the Holy Spirit says: "Today, if you will hear His voice, do not harden your hearts as in the rebellion, in the day of trial in the wilderness, where your fathers tested Me, tried Me, and saw My works forty years. Therefore I was angry with that generation, and said, 'They always go astray in their heart, and they have not known My ways.' So I swore in My wrath 'They shall not enter My rest.'"

Frequently, the writer of Hebrews, when introducing a quote from the Old Testament—uses the expression, "God says," or "The Holy Spirit says." The fact is—*God* is the author of the Scriptures; *men* were the writers.

---

[45]   Most commentators (including MacArthur, Wiersbe, Wuest, Vine, etc.) say, in essence, that "those who do not *continue* were never in the house at all."

The words in verses 7b-11 are quoted from Psalm 95, but what the Psalmist wrote was not his own opinion, nor his own choice of words. When David wrote the words, the Holy Spirit was speaking (verse 7a). The Holy Spirit was involved in writing every word of Scripture and this is one argument for the trustworthiness of Scripture.

The word "Today" (verse 7) has a sense of urgency about it. The reference is not to yesterday; yesterday is gone. When God confronts the human heart, it is always for action now—not tomorrow, not next week, not next year. Today is God's time. "Now is the day of salvation" (2 Corinthians 6:2b). Do it now! Do not wait until another time! The word *today* is used again in verses 13 and 15.[46]

This section quotes Psalm 95:7b-11 in order to compare the experience of Israel with that of the church. The church today must not repeat the failure which Israel experienced.

The "rebellion" ["temptation" KJV][47] (verse 8) mentioned here is a reference to the occasion described in Exodus 17:1-7 when the people were thirsty and Moses struck the rock, which then flowed abundantly with water. The judgment that fell upon the people of Israel (verse 11) is described in Numbers 14:20-38, where the Israelites, who were at the very edge of the Promised Land, had to turn back and

---

[46] John MacArthur reminds readers that in his earlier ministry, D. L. Moody often would end his evangelistic messages with the words "Go home and think about what I've said." One night, in Chicago, he told the people to do this and to come back the next night ready to make a decision. But one of the nights when Moody had made that statement, was the night when the Chicago fire broke out and some who had been in his audience died. That was the last time that D. L. Moody told anyone to think about the claims of Christ and make a decision later (*New Testament Commentary: Hebrews,* page 75).

[47] Kenneth Wuest says that the Greek word translated "rebellion" is *peirasmos*, preceded here by the definite article, and thus points to a particular temptation. The primary meaning of the word is "to put to a test" (*Hebrews in the Greek New Testament*, page 75).

wander in the desert until all who were 20 years and older would die (except for Joshua and Caleb).

The *hardening of hearts* takes place whenever individuals reject God's call. Many today have the idea that they can be saved whenever they get ready, but that is not true. We are to call upon God "while He is near" (Isaiah 55:6), for God's Spirit will not always call (Genesis 6:3b).[48] For more on the hardening of hearts, see the comments under verse 13.

Israel apparently forgot all the miracles God had done in order to bring them safely out of the land of Egypt, and now their refusal to go and take the land of Canaan angered the Lord (verse 10a). God says "they always go astray[49] in their heart, and they have not known My ways" (verse 10b). Yet they had seen God's miracles in their behalf (verse 9b). They saw *the sea stand up in heaps* to let them cross the waters on dry land. They saw *the manna* morning after morning lying like dew throughout the entire camp. They saw *the waters gushing forth* from the rock when Moses smote it. They saw *Mount Sinai covered with the fire of God's presence.* But they failed to lay hold of God's message in all this—and so God determined that none of those who disbelieved should enter the land which he had promised to their fathers—a land which He called "My rest" (verse 11).

b. Unbelief will prevent entering the rest (3:12-19)

The writer now warns readers, that just as the Israelites failed to enter Canaan through unbelief, they too will miss a similar blessing if they do not continue in the faith.

---

[48] The gospel song says, "There's a line that is drawn by rejecting the Lord, where the call of His Spirit is lost; as you hurry along with the pleasure-mad throng, have you counted, have you counted the cost?"

[49] The people's sins are described as hardening their hearts (verse 8), testing God (verse 9), going astray (verse 10), being disobedient (verse 18), and unbelieving (verse 19).

(3:12-14) Beware, brethren, lest there be in any of you an evil heart of unbelief in departing from the living God; but exhort one another daily, while it is called "Today," lest any of you be hardened through the deceitfulness of sin. For we have become partakers of Christ if we hold the beginning of our confidence steadfast to the end,

The terms "holy brethren" (verse 1), and "brethren" (verse 12) indicate that the readers were Christians. The call now is given to each individual to examine his own heart. They departed "from the living God."[50] The primary problem these people had was *unbelief.* They failed to take to heart the commands and promises which God had given.

Believers are in continual need of encouragement and exhortation. God's people are to meet with one another from time to time and "exhort one another daily" (verse 13a). The Greek word translated "exhort" (*parakleite*) is a word used to describe the military commander who encourages and strengthens his soldiers before an upcoming battle. Every member of the body of Christ should make it a point to try and find opportunities for speaking uplifting words, and for bringing cheerful encouragement to other brothers and sisters in the faith.

Verse 13b continues by stating clearly that the human heart can become "hardened" through the deceitfulness of sin. One of the reasons why the great majority of those who are saved, have made the decision for Christ in the days of their youth—is that the young person has the advantage of a tender heart. The child has a tender conscience, and is easily moved by the fear of punishment; the child knows that it is dangerous to go on in sin. But those *who continue on* in sin,

---

[50] W. E. Vine says, "The 'living God' sometimes stands in contrast to idols; here it suggests His immortality and greatness, as in Hebrews 9:14, 10:31, and 12:22" (*The Epistle to the Hebrews*, page 36).

and ignore the call of the Holy Spirit, will find that their hearts become more calloused and accustomed to sin.

Every brazen infidel who is alive today, was once a tender-hearted child that may have trembled at the very thought of his sin—but delay has hardened his heart. Every drunkard was once an innocent child—likely loved by his parents with a promising future. Every painted prostitute was once a sweet-faced little girl, precious and gentle, with holy possibilities—but now the passing days of unrebuked sin in her life have led to indifference about holy matters. The little child born into this world with bright eyes and happy smiles and a sweet disposition—gradually becomes hardened by the deceitfulness of sin.

It seems that the readers of Hebrews were considering turning from Christianity back to Judaism. The writer makes it clear that merely *beginning* the Christian life is not enough. We must *continue* living in loyalty to Christ (verse 14).The faith that saves is a faith that lays hold of God and never lets go. Those who hold on in confidence, steadfastly unto the end, will experience *the rest* prepared for God's people.

(3:15-19) while it is said: "Today, if you will hear His voice, do not harden your hearts as in the rebellion." For who, having heard, rebelled? Indeed, was it not all who came out of Egypt, led by Moses? Now with whom was He angry forty years? Was it not with those who sinned, whose corpses fell in the wilderness? And to whom did He swear that they would not enter His rest, but to those who did not obey? So we see that they could not enter in because of unbelief.

The writer of Hebrews once again (in verse 15) refers to Psalm 95. The people of Israel had continued to rebel until God sentenced them to wander in the wilderness for the 40 years until the rebellious generation had died.

Verse 16 speaks of the extent of their rebellion. All the

50

Jews who had come out of Egypt (except Caleb and Joshua) joined in the rebellion. Verse 17 draws attention to the 40 years of wandering. There were 603,550 men who left Egypt (Numbers 1:46), and it can be assumed that there were an equal number of women who were twenty years old or older. Therefore the entire group was likely more than two million people. This means that about 90 adults *died each day* during the years in the wilderness. Day after day the desert was littered with more corpses, as those who had been given to unbelief "fell" (verse 17b).

Those who were told that they could not enter "His rest" were the ones who refused to hear the voice of God. They chose not to obey (verse 18), and they are the ones "whose corpses fell in the wilderness" (verse 17b).

The concluding verse of the section (verse 19), is an indirect warning to the readers, reminding them to learn from the sins of their forefathers.

c. Exhortations to claim and enter the rest (4:1-11)

The "rest" which God promises does not refer to the weekly Sabbath rest, nor is it the "rest" given to some of Israel under the leadership of Joshua in the Land of Canaan. The "rest" which is presented in 4:9 is *the rest* which will be realized in Heaven, the eternal home of the redeemed.[51]

(4:1-11) Therefore, since a promise remains of entering His rest, let us fear lest any of you seem to have come short of it. For indeed the gospel was preached to us as well as to them; but the word which they heard did not profit them, not being mixed with faith in those who heard it. For we who have be-

---

[51] L. W. Teeter, writing in 1894, expressed the typical early Brethren view of *the rest* spoken about in Hebrews 4. He says, "*His rest* is the rest which God has prepared for the faithful, and which they shall enter at the close of their earthly pilgrimage—heaven. This is the rest for the spiritual man, while the earthly Canaan was the resting-place for the natural man (Deuteronomy 12:9-10), and was only a type of the spiritual" (*New Testament Commentary*, page 366).

lieved do enter that rest, as He has said: "So I swore in My wrath, 'They shall not enter My rest,'" although the works were finished from the foundation of the world. For He has spoken in a certain place of the seventh day in this way: "And God rested on the seventh day from all His works"; and again in this place: "They shall not enter My rest." Since therefore it remains that some must enter it, and those to whom it was first preached did not enter because of disobedience, again He designates a certain day, saying in David, "Today," after such a long time, as it has been said: "Today, if you will hear His voice, Do not harden your hearts." For if Joshua had given them rest, then He would not afterward have spoken of another day. There remains therefore a rest for the people of God. For he who has entered His rest has himself also ceased from his works as God did from His. Let us therefore be diligent to enter that rest, lest anyone fall according to the same example of disobedience.

These verses explain the nature and certainty of the rest God has promised His people, and the disappointing tragedy of any believer's failure to enter into it (verse 1).

The early Christians[52] (as well as the Christians today) have heard good news proclaimed; the wilderness generation also heard good news (verse 2a).[53] Those who believe the message now, are in the process of entering the rest God has prepared (verse 3a). Those *who rebelled in the past* were indeed prohibited from entering the place of rest (verse 2b). Those *who do not now* receive the gospel message by an act of faith, also fall short of entering the rest (verse 3b).

---

[52]   Christians today should follow the example of the early believers at Thessalonica (1 Thessalonians 2:13).

[53]   One of the most important questions in life is "How may an unholy people approach a holy God?" The book of Leviticus shows that the way to God is by *sacrifice*, and the daily walk with God is by *separation*. The sacrifices described in Leviticus depicted to the people of Israel how *the shedding of the blood of a substitute* placated the righteous displeasure of God.

What is "that rest" (verse 3)? It is *primarily* a future place of blessedness where the saved will walk with God in the eternal world. The enjoyment of God's rest is for those who believe, not for those who choose the way of unbelief.

The "rest" promised in Hebrews 4:3 refers to a future heavenly rest, and to a present rest of faith. The *future heavenly rest* speaks of a time when the toils and labors of this life are ended. The promise in Revelation 14:13 is that those who die in the Lord "may *rest* from their labors and their works follow them." The *present rest of faith* speaks of a freedom that comes from joyful surrender to the Lord, who said, "Take My yoke upon you and learn from Me, for I am gentle and lowly in heart, and you will find *rest* for your souls" (Matthew 11:29).

The concept of rest is illustrated in verse 4. When God rested on the seventh day, He completed the work of creation, but He did not just take a day off eternally. Rest, for God, did not mean idleness, for He continues the work of sustaining life on the earth. And just so, those who rest with Jesus find God's blessing and peace—but not a cessation of labor. Our rest with God gives new strength, but it does not mean mere inactivity. Heaven will be a place of rest, but it will not consist of listless laziness.

The exact reference for the quote in verses 4 and 5 is not given; this indicates that the writer of Hebrews was certain that the readers were familiar with the message of the Old Testament.[54] Disobedience prevented multitudes from entering the Canaan rest (verse 6). And although some did enter with Joshua, there was conflict in Canaan, and there-

---

[54] The words, "God rested on the seventh day from all His works" (verse 4), mean that He enjoyed the satisfaction and repose that comes with the completion of a task. Rest, for God, does not mean idleness; it was simply a cessation from the work of creation (Genesis 2:2).

fore it was not a restful experience (verse 8).

Verse 7 repeats the warning spelled out in Hebrews 3:7b-11.[55] The real rest still awaits the people of God (verse 9). Those who fully enter the rest which God has prepared will have responded to God's voice, and will have ceased from their earthly tasks and activities, just as God rested from His works of creation (verse 10).

The *rest* promised to the Children of Israel was only figurative of a much greater rest yet to come. But in light of what happened to the Israelites who failed to enter in because of unbelief, followers of Christ need to be careful not to displease the Lord by doubt and unbelief. Christians are exhorted to put forth every effort to enter into the rest which God has prepared, and are warned not to fail because of disobedience (verse 11).

The rest which God promises, then, is something worth laboring for. We should give all diligence to enter into it.

d. Unbelief never goes undetected (4:12-13)

The writer of Hebrews makes a turn of thought in verses 12 and 13. One can smooth over his outward actions, but no one can hide from God the real purpose or intent of the heart.

(4:12) For the word of God is living and powerful, and sharper than any two-edged sword, piercing even to the division of soul and spirit, and of joints and marrow, and is a discerner of the thoughts and intents of the heart.

The "word of God is living and powerful" (verse 12a). It is a living thing; it is not a dead book. Those who preach and proclaim the Word of God, are never wasting their time, because God's Word is alive and it will accomplish its pur-

---

[55] The Psalm 95 passage is introduced in 3:7 by attributing the words to the Holy Spirit. The same passage is introduced in 4:7 by attributing the words to David. When we carefully interpret Scripture we are not merely expressing our own opinions; we are explaining the message of God!

pose; God's word "shall not return to Me void, but it shall accomplish what I please" (Isaiah 55:11). Man's word may be educational and instructive, but it has no life.

The Word of God is not only *living*, but it is also *powerful*. The word "powerful" is translated from the Greek *energes*, from which the English word "energy" is derived. Psalm 119:11 declares that God's Word is to be hidden in the heart so that we might not sin against the Lord. The powerful Word can sanctify and cleanse (Ephesians 5:26).

God's Word is "sharper than any two-edged sword" (verse 12a). It cuts into the unspoken thoughts and reveals hidden ideas one may hold from time to time.[56] Those persons who do not want to know about themselves and what lies deeply rooted inside, should stay away from the Bible!

God's Word can discern "the thoughts and intents of the heart." It distinguishes between "soul and spirit" and "joints and marrow" (verse 12b). The Word of God penetrates the human frame, and divides asunder the soul and spirit, separating that which pertains to self, and that which pertains to God.[57] It can discriminate between the individual who lives only in *the realm of the soul* (satisfied with mere physical and aesthetic pursuits), and the one whose *spirit has been made alive* to the things of God by regeneration.

Almost every household in the United States has a Bible; we must never forget Who speaks through its pages, and we must never handle God's Word irreverently, carelessly, or

---

[56] Menno Simons referred to the Word of God *as a sharp sword* when he spoke about biblical nonresistance. He said, "Iron and metal...swords we leave to those who (unfortunately) see human blood and swine's blood as of nearly equal value." [Simons then referred to the sword of the Spirit in Luke 11:28 and Hebrews 4:12] (*Spiritual Life in Anabaptism*, Cornelius J. Dyck, page 113).

[57] John Phillips says, "A person may weep at the Lord's Table or shout his hallelujahs at the testimony meeting; however, his emotions may be carnal just as easily as spiritual" (*Exploring Hebrews*, page 78).

lightly. We must guard against reading the Word, and laying it down untouched by its appeal to the heart.

(4:13) And there is no creature hidden from His sight, but all things are naked and open to the eyes of Him to whom we must give account.

God knows absolutely everything about us. When the woman at the well spoke with Jesus and made a commitment to receive Him, she went back to the city and said, "Come, see a Man who told me all things that I ever did" (John 4:29). Our lives are an open book before the Lord Jesus. The ancient proverb says that God can even see a black ant crawling on a black rock on a black night!

We must always remember that the One who sees all is constantly watching.[58] Proverbs 15:3 says that "the eyes of the Lord are in every place, keeping watch on the evil and the good." A church building in France has a *huge painting of an eye* on the ceiling over the worshiping congregation, as a reminder of the omniscience of God.

The main focus in Hebrews 4 is not so much on the unbelieving Israelites who in Old Testament times refused to obey God. The focus is primarily on believers in this age who by faith choose to enter God's rest. The unbelieving Hebrews failed to listen to God's voice, and as a result perished on the way to the land God had promised. Christians who look soberly at God's Word are alerted to the serious dangers of unbelief, and will be inspired to keep on in the Christian life until they reach God's eternal rest.

---

[58] The Emperor of China in early years was said to have 80,000 eyes. On the Great Wall of China there were 40,000 watchtowers, and a guard was in each tower day and night to defend the safety of China. This was the greatest example of human vigilance ever known in the world—but it was only human watchfulness subject to human frailty.

Chapter 4

CHRIST IS THE SUPERIOR HIGH PRIEST
Hebrews 4:14—5:10

This section of the book of Hebrews deals with *the work* of Christ in the present age. The writer explains the meaning of the resurrection and the ascension of Christ, highlighting especially His work as a High Priest.

1. Christ is Superior in His Priesthood (4:14-16)

The early chapters of the book of Acts explain that forty days after His resurrection, Jesus ascended into heaven to take up His work of being an Advocate for God's people.

The exalted *position* of Christ has been described in the first few chapters of Hebrews. Now, beginning with Hebrews 4:14, the reader is given details about the present high priestly *work* of the Lord Jesus.

The "priest" was the official worship-leader in the nation Israel. He represented the people before God,[59] and conducted various rituals to atone for their sins. This priestly function in earliest times was carried out by the father of a family (Job 1:5) or by the head of a tribe—until the days of Moses and Aaron. When Israel was called out as a nation, Aaron was appointed the first high priest, and thus the office of priesthood was formally established (Exodus 28:1).

---

[59] It is the universal sinfulness of man which makes the priesthood necessary. The sacrifices offered up by the priests, symbolize the means by which reconciliation between sinful human beings and their holy Creator can be effected. The animal which was slain in the sinner's stead, symbolized the transference of the individual's sin to an innocent victim. This pictured atonement by the substitutionary death of an innocent victim—but the death of an irrational brute beast could never be a proper substitute for man. The writer of Hebrews says that it is not possible that the blood of bulls and goats could take away sin (10:4).

The one main characteristic of a priest is that he has access with God, and thus brings sacrifices to the Lord. In Old Testament times, this access to God was the privilege only of the high priest, who once a year would enter into the Most Holy Place of the Temple, and there speak with God on behalf of the people. The high priests had to offer sacrifices for his own sins and then also for the sins of the people.

On the Day of Atonement, the high priest bathed, changed into a linen garment, and placed his hand upon the head of a young bull which was brought to the brazen altar as a sacrifice (Leviticus 16:4). He recited his own sins with his hands over the head of the animal. He then sacrificed the bull, took its blood into the Holy of Holies (located at the innermost part of the Temple). Along with the blood of the bull he took a pair of goats.

The high priest then offered a second sacrifice (one of the two goats) which he sacrificed for the sins of the people. Then the high priest placed his hands upon the other goat, and that animal became a "scapegoat" (as it was called), and it was led through the crowd of people to a place out in the wilderness—and there it was set free. (Read about it in Leviticus 16:8, 10, and 26).

Those sacrifices made satisfaction for sin for another year. The next year, on the Day of Atonement (*Yom Kippur*, as it is called in our day), the sacrifices needed to be repeated all over again (Hebrews 10:1-4). The endless repetition of the sacrifices offered by the priests demonstrated the inadequacy of those sacrifices to deal fully with sin.

Jesus, by way of contrast, had no need to offer sacrifices for Himself, for He had no sin (Hebrews 7:27-28). The human priests offered animal blood which could never *permanently* take away sin (Hebrews 10:1-4), but Jesus offered His own blood which indeed cleanses from all sin (Hebrews

9:12; 1 John 1:7). The purpose of the old order of priest-hood was to teach the people that atonement for sins requires the provision of an innocent victim in place of the sinner. And even though the Levitical order could not accomplish this atonement permanently, it did keep alive the coming of a perfect Sacrifice for human sin.[60]

The high priest was bound to a higher degree of ritual purity than ordinary Levitical priests. He could have no contact with dead bodies, including the bodies of his own parents. He could not marry a widow, a harlot, or a woman who had been divorced. He was allowed to marry only an Israelite virgin (Leviticus 21:10-15).

In Hebrews 4:14-16 the writer makes three statements (listed below) about our High Priest, the Lord Jesus Christ. Only in Hebrews is Jesus said to be a High Priest. First, there is a reference to the present priestly work of Jesus.

a. The priesthood of Jesus (4:14)

(4:14) Seeing then that we have a great High Priest who has passed through the heavens, Jesus the Son of God, let us hold fast our confession.

Jesus is presently our High Priest in Heaven. He "passed through the heavens"—a reference to His triumphant ascension into Heaven. The writer twice says that He "sat down at the right hand" of God (Hebrews 1:3; 10:12). His ascension and being seated at the right hand of God are guarantees that His work for mankind is finished, and that it was complete and satisfactory to the heavenly Father. The word "great" ("a

---

[60] For Christians, Jesus Christ is understood to be the perfect High Priest (Hebrews 5:5-9; Hebrews 6:20). He took upon Himself the sins of the world, and He is the Mediator of a new covenant between God and those who choose to serve the Lord. His one sacrifice was made once for all, and no longer was there any need for the annual ritual on the Day of Atonement, and no longer must sacrifices be repeated year after year.

great High Priest") indicates that Jesus is superior to the earthly high priests described in the Old Testament. *They* entered into God's presence (the innermost part in the Temple) once a year on the Day of Atonement. By way of contrast, *Jesus* entered the heavens and sat down, and is always in the presence of God interceding for His people. When Jesus sat down in the presence of God, the Majesty on High said, *"I'm satisfied! My Son Jesus accomplished the atonement for all those who come to Him by faith, and I accept what He did for them."* Surely with such a great High Priest ministering on our behalf, we do not want to give up our profession of faith.

The fact that Jesus ascended into Heaven and sat down at the right hand of the Father means that His saving work is finished. It happened "once at the end of the ages" (Hebrews 9:26). The ascension of Christ was not just the dramatic end of His earthly ministry. It was God's guarantee that the work of Jesus on the cross did indeed satisfactorily purchase our redemption.

b. *The compassion of Christ (4:15)*

Many people seem to think of God as far removed from human life and from our human concerns. But verse 15 says that when we reach out to God in faith, we can *touch* Him (KJV)! He can be reached when we come to Him in believing prayer.

(4:15) For we do not have a High Priest who cannot sympathize with our weaknesses, but was in all points tempted as we are, yet without sin.

When we are troubled and hurt and despondent, we like to share our feelings and needs with someone who understands. The sentence in one of our hymns which says, "No one understands like Jesus"—is really a very true statement. He experienced the same kinds of disappointments and grief and frustrations that all of us at times experience. Because

Jesus is the Son of God, some might be inclined to question whether Christ really understands our human predicament, or whether He is really interested in the problems of just one ordinary person.

But it is not that way at all. Jesus is a merciful and faithful High Priest who suffered when He was here on earth. In His human body He was tempted like we are. It is true that He never sinned, but He can sympathize with us. Verse 15 says, "We do not have a High Priest who cannot sympathize with our weaknesses."[61] The Lord Jesus is full of sympathy and of tender compassion. Just because He is in Heaven, and because He is the mighty Son of God, does not remove Him from understanding our human needs.

Jesus knows what it is like to be tempted. As a man on earth, Jesus did not live in isolation from human temptation. He was tempted just as intensely as we are.[62] He experienced hunger, weariness, and pain. When His back was lacerated and bleeding from the scourging (just before He went to the cross), His enemies put a purple robe on Him and placed a rod in His right hand. The rod was a staff like a king carries as a symbol of his authority. Then they mocked Him and said, "Hail, *king* of the Jews."

Not only the soldiers, but the chief priests, and the onlookers—all were making fun of Him while He was in pain. All humans know that it is hard to be in pain and then have people laugh at them. The Bible says that we should follow His example (1 Peter 2:21).

---

[61] The KJV rendering describes Jesus *as not* One who "cannot be touched with the feeling of our infirmities." The double negative (used in most translations) is merely another way of saying that He *does* sympathize with our feelings.

[62] We can never say that temptation was easier for Jesus. The only person who knows the full force of a particular temptation, is the one who resists it to the end—and refuses to give in. Those who give in at some point along the way do not know *the fierceness* of the temptation that would follow at a later point.

Jesus faced all the basic trials of life. He knows what it is like to experience infirmities of various kinds,[63] and with tender compassion He is touched by our needs. He was tempted like we are, and so He understands and looks upon us with loving kindness.

J. C. Macauley tells about a boy who had lost his right hand, and he was so humiliated that he wanted *no one* to see him. When his father suggested the possibility of bringing a minister friend of his to come and see him—the boy objected. The father, however, followed his own counsel and invited the minister to their home. As the visitor entered the house, the boy noticed that *he* also had *no right hand*. There was an immediate bond of sympathy between the two—and when the minister said, "I know how it feels"—the boy *knew* he had a friend indeed.

c. The boldness of believers (4:16)

The disciple of Jesus is urged to come to God in prayer, and to come with great confidence.

(4:16) Let us...come boldly to the throne of grace, that we may obtain mercy and find grace to help in time of need.

Since our High Priest is at the right hand of God interceding for us, we have the freedom of access to the very throne of God at any time. We are to approach the throne of grace boldly, and tell the Lord about our trials—and we can be sure that God will show His favor in our behalf.

This passage encourages us to pray with a great deal of confidence. The "throne of grace" refers to the throne of God. To "come boldly" means literally "Come, saying all." Come

---

[63] Jesus was not tempted in *every particular*. He was not tempted as a father, or as a property owner, or as an employer. Jesus never had a flat tire; He never got caught in an airplane in a snowstorm. But many of those things are various forms of frustration, and Jesus did meet His share of frustrations. He was tempted in *all areas* that we are—including the lust of the flesh, the lust of the eyes, and the pride of life, as described in 1 John 2:16.

as you are. Say what you feel. Ask what you need. Pour out your fears. Confess your wandering thoughts. The tense of the word "come" means that we are to come constantly, repeatedly, and continually.

When Jesus died and was buried, and rose again, and then ascended into heaven to become our great High Priest, the way to God was opened up, and the invitation to every believer is "Come, and find the grace and help that you need—find it at the altar of prayer."[64] Our need may be material, physical, or spiritual. Believers who call boldly on the name of the Lord will discover that He hears and answers.

Prayerlessness is really a great sin. Those who do not devote time each day to earnest, believing prayer—in essence are saying that they can cope with life without divine help. Prayerlessness is human arrogance at its worst. Prayerlessness is really a form of practical atheism. Prayerlessness in the Christian life says that we believe in God, but we

---

[64] A night-attendant in a city drug store tells about a thrilling answer to prayer. The large drug stores in the city are often open all night in order to fill prescriptions. The night-attendant sleeps on a couch at the rear of the store. Customers ring a buzzer if they want service. The attendant, who gave testimony to God's faithfulness, was just about sleeping one cold and dismal night many years ago in New York City—when he was aroused by the buzzer. When he answered the door, it was a little boy. *"Please mister, get this medicine quick, my mommy is awfully sick."* Sleepily and hurriedly he filled the prescription—and the boy was off. After he had gone, the attendant put away the bottles of medicine, and recorded the prescription—*only to notice (to his horror) that he had given the boy a deadly poison, and not the medicine he had intended to give.* The attendant didn't know which way the boy had gone. It was raining and dark outside. He looked in the phone book, but the name was not there. So he went to his cot, fell on his knees, and asked God to overrule this tragic mistake for His glory—and then he lay down again on the cot. It was not long until the buzzer rang again, and when he answered, it was the same boy. He was crying frantically. He said, "Mister, I was running to get this medicine home to my mommy as quick as I could—and I slipped and fell and broke the bottle. Will you please get the medicine for me again?" It is obvious that God over-ruled even a careless mistake, to answer the fervent prayer of a humble man of God.

can get along without Him. Hebrews 4:16 urges us to come into the presence of God, for God is one who welcomes us, and Christ is one who understands us.[65]

God answers our prayers in one of three ways. *Eliezer* (the servant of Abraham) was given a quick "yes." *Paul* (requesting the removal of the thorn) was told "no." *Moses* (who wanted to see the Promised Land) had to "wait."

Each of the answers was given in kindness—intended for the benefit of the one who prayed. God *does* answer prayer, and sometimes He answers in most unusual ways.

The closing verses of Hebrews 4 contain some precious words of encouragement. They tell us about one of the provisions which God in His grace provides for us while we are still in this place of testing. Jesus serves as our great High Priest (our advocate). He pleads our cause. He stands ready to meet our needs—but He expects us to be brave—and come to Him and ask in simple faith.

Christians have heard many appeals to prayer. We know that speaking with God is a valuable privilege. But prayer, on a regular basis, is hard work—and as a result, genuine intercessory prayer is often neglected. The promise here should call each follower of Christ to a greater commitment in the area of faithful prayer.

---

[65]   One morning in Stuttgart, Germany during World War 2, a lady named Irmgart Wood (and her mother) saw an American plane catch fire and fall from the sky. Instinctively, she and her mother prayed for the pilot—even though he was flying an American plane (and Americans were considered enemies of Germany). It was years later that the two women migrated to America and settled on the West Coast. Irmgard's mother got a job in a hospital in California. And one day a patient in the hospital heard her German accent, and said to her, "Where did you live in Germany?" "Stuttgart," she said. The patient said, *"I almost got killed in Stuttgart during World War 2. My plane caught fire one morning and fell from the sky. Somebody must have been praying for me."* Readers can guess the conversation that followed. To fail to start the day with prayer—says in essence that *we can cope with life* without divine aid.

2. Christ is Superior in His Qualifications (5:1-10)

Hebrews 5 outlines the general qualifications for the office of high priest in Israel, and shows that Jesus possessed those qualifications. The first four verses of the chapter describe in more detail the office of the earthly priest. The qualifications for high priests are stated in these verses.

a. The office of the high priest (5:1-4)

(5:1-4) For every high priest taken from among men is appointed for men in things pertaining to God, that he may offer both gifts and sacrifices for sins. He can have compassion on those who are ignorant and going astray, since he himself is also subject to weakness. Because of this he is required as for the people, so also for himself, to offer sacrifices for sins. And no man takes this honor to himself, but he who is called by God, just as Aaron was.

The high priest in Israel was ordained by God to offer gifts and sacrifices (see 8:3) for himself and for others. He was to be from the family of Aaron (Exodus 28:1). His task was to represent sinful human beings before God (verse 1).

The high priest was to be a man who had compassion for sinners, one who would deal gently with others—and he was able to have that compassion because he was aware of his own weaknesses (verse 2). But the fact that he was imperfect and easily fell into sin too, meant that he was required to offer sacrifices for his own sins[66] as well as for the sins of the people (verse 3).

The priest in Israel *did not appoint himself* to be a priest. He was to be "called by God" (verse 4). He was not to view the office as something he would choose for himself as a vocation. The high priest was to be one who received a di-

---

[66] Consider the weakness of Aaron: he gave a feeble excuse to Moses for yielding to the demands of the people for a *visible* god to worship. He said, "So they gave [their gold] to me, and I cast it into the fire, and this calf came out" (Exodus 32:24).

vine call to the office (verse 4). To minister on behalf of others as high priest, was such a great honor that he could be a high priest only if God called him to the task. This may be one of the reasons why the early Anabaptists frowned upon volunteering for the ministry without receiving an official call from the church.[67]

b. Christ's qualifications for high priest (5:5-10)

This section explains the relation between Christ and the order of Aaron. At the same time, it also introduces the priesthood of Melchizedek.

(5:5-10) So also Christ did not glorify Himself to become High Priest, but it was He who said to Him: "You are My Son, today I have begotten You." As He also says in another place: "You are a priest forever according to the order of Melchizedek"; who, in the days of His flesh, when He had offered up prayers and supplications, with vehement cries and tears to Him who was able to save Him from death, and was heard because of His godly fear, though He was a Son, yet He learned obedience by the things which He suffered. And having been perfected, He became the author of eternal salvation to all who obey Him, called by God as High Priest "according to the order of Melchizedek,"

Christ did not take upon Himself the glory of becoming a high priest. Jesus was *divinely called* by the heavenly Father (verse 5). The author of Hebrews quotes from Psalm 2:7, and then from Psalm 110:4 to support that truth (verse 6).

Not only was Jesus divinely called, but He was *personally fit* for the high priesthood. The leading idea in this section is that our Lord's sufferings qualified Him perfectly to be the author of salvation (verses 7-10). The human

---

[67]   J. C. Macaulay comments: "It was a sin of sacrilege and presumption for any one to intrude into the priest's office. Korah and his brethren presumed and were destroyed in the presence of all the people. Uzziah presumed and was smitten with leprosy" (*Expository Commentary on Hebrews*, page 68).

priests from the family of Aaron could sympathize with other humans because they, too, were prone to sin. Jesus could sympathize even more effectively, because suffering is a very skilled teacher, and gives one a sense of compassion for others who are hurting.

Christ's "strong crying and tears" (verse 7, KJV) most likely describe the intensity of the Lord's grief in the Garden of Gethsemane. See also John 12:27. The words, "[He] was heard because of His godly fear" (verse 7b) have puzzled Bible readers. It is helpful to note that the word translated "fear" is not *phobos*, the ordinary word for fear, but is instead, *eulabeias*, a word which speaks of respect,[68] and not of a cringing kind of fear. Jesus did not have a fear of physical death, but the weight of the world's sorrow was bearing down upon His soul, and the darkness of the world's sin was wrapping around Him. The horror of the world's rebellion and disrespect for God was gripping Him.

The statement that Jesus "learned obedience by the things which He suffered" (verse 8b) is also puzzling to the general Bible reader. Why would Jesus, the omniscient One need *to learn* anything?[69] He had never been disobedient, nor had He ever even been disposed to disobey. For Jesus, obedience to the heavenly Father had always been a delight (Psalm 40:8; John 6:38).

The statement in verse 8 does not mean that Jesus turned from disobedience to obedience—but that He obeyed God in a way that He had never done before, even when He

---

[68]   The word *eulabeias* means "circumspect, full of reverence toward God, devout, pious" (*Analytical Greek Lexicon*, page 174). Even as a youth, the thing that mattered to Jesus more than anything else, was His concern about living in obedient surrender to God's will (Luke 2:49, 52).

[69]   Christians should acknowledge that a divine mystery is involved in the idea of Jesus *learning obedience*. It is difficult to understand why the divine Son would need to learn.

experienced suffering and pain as a human being. He continued to obey God even in the midst of suffering.

The term in verse 9, "having been perfected" (or "being made perfect" [KJV]) also seems awkward to the casual reader. But to say that Jesus was "made perfect" does not suggest that He was imperfect before He suffered. The Greek word translated "perfect" is *teleiotheis*, which describes perfection in terms of *completeness*. After passing victoriously through suffering—the redemptive plan was complete, and Jesus became the source of eternal salvation "to all who obey Him" (verse 9).[70] The agonies of soul which Jesus experienced in Gethsemane, and on the cross of Calvary, qualified Him as a high priest to sympathize with people who are suffering.

Jesus Christ is a Priest, not after the order of Aaron, but after the order of Melchizedek (verse 10). That concept will be developed further when we study Hebrews 7, but there is one observation that can be made here.

Jesus could never have been a Levitical priest because He was born of the tribe of Judah (Hebrews 7:14), and not of the tribe of Levi. Thus Jesus must be associated with another order of priests—that of Melchizedek.

---

[70] Dale Stoffer quotes Alexander Mack as saying that "if faith is to be saving faith, it 'must be proved by love and obedience.'" Stoffer explains that one of Mack's Scriptural basis for that teaching is seen in the example of Jesus submitting Himself to God's will in Hebrews 5:7-9 (*Background of Brethren Doctrines*, page 76). Obedience is stressed throughout the Bible. When Peter and the other apostles spoke of repentance and the forgiveness of sins, they spoke of the *"Holy Spirit, whom God has given to those who obey Him"* (Acts 5:32). The word "obey" is likely the most important single word in the Bible.

Chapter 5

WARNING: THE DANGER OF IMMATURITY
Hebrews 5:11—6:20

This section of the book of Hebrews *contains the third warning passage of the book*. The first warning passage is in 2:1-4, warning about the danger of neglect. The second warning passage is in 3:7—4:13, warning about the danger of unbelief. The writer now warns against the danger of spiritual immaturity and falling away from faith in Christ.

1. Failure to Progress in the Faith (5:11-14)

The writer of Hebrews has just stated that Christ is a High Priest "according to the order of Melchizedek" (verse 10). The opening words of this section ("of whom") refer back to Melchizedek.

(5:11-14) of whom we have much to say, and hard to explain, since you have become dull of hearing. For though by this time you ought to be teachers, you need someone to teach you again the first principles of the oracles of God; and you have come to need milk and not solid food. For everyone who partakes only of milk is unskilled in the word of righteousness, for he is a babe. But solid food belongs to those who are of full age, that is, those who by reason of use have their senses exercised to discern both good and evil.

The writer realized that the subject was a difficult one to explain. He had many things to say about this little known Old Testament character, but the believers to whom he was writing had become "dull of hearing" (verse 11). So the writer issued strong words, rebuking those who were sluggish and "dull of hearing." Many Christians in the same way seem to be satisfied with an imperfect and inadequate knowledge of God and His Word.

Probably some of the Hebrew Christians (verse 12a) posed as teachers, but they were not really qualified to teach the Word. That was the case in 1 Timothy 1:7, where the Apostle Paul speaks of those who desire "to be teachers of the law, [but] understanding neither what they say nor the things which they affirm." The task of teaching requires knowledge of the Word (verse 13), and the ability to discern things that are good and evil (verse 14).

Some believers are babies who need milk (verse 12b), that is, the simple plain message of God's truth. Some, such as the early Hebrew Christians, need to be taught the basics over and over again because they so easily forget what they have learned. The writer of Hebrews reprimands such persons for not becoming mature adults in Christ.

The "milk" phase refers to the beginning level of instruction for Christians (the ABCs of the Word);[71] the "solid food" phase describes advanced instruction. Both the milk phase and the solid food phase are very important, but those who never reached the solid food stage are seriously lacking. One of our 27 grandchildren (at the time of this writing) is just learning to walk—and that is an important stage—but if he stays at that level we know that something is defective.

2. Exhortations to Make Spiritual Progress (6:1-3)

Some of the Hebrew readers were still magnifying the elementary teachings of the Christian faith and were not moving on to the meat of the Word of God.

(6:1-3) Therefore, leaving the discussion of the elementary principles of Christ, let us go on to perfection, not laying again the foundation of repentance from dead works and of

---

[71] The writer does not mean that the more simple teachings are to be forgotten or denied or neglected, but that attention is not to be limited to them. We learn the alphabet as a foundation, but we do not remain there.

faith toward God, of the doctrine of baptisms, of laying on of hands, of resurrection of the dead, and of eternal judgment. And this we will do if God permits.

The mention of "leaving" the discussion of the elementary principles (verse 1a) does not mean deserting them.

The call, "let us go on to perfection" (verse 1b), is not referring to a state of *perfect moral attainment*, but a call to move on to a greater maturity in knowledge and application of God's Word. The writer wants those who are immature in Christ to grow into a greater level of maturity. To do this, believers must remember six foundational principles, but they must move beyond the principles, to some of the practical aspects of Christian living. Some Christians never seem to reach beyond first grade when it comes to the deeper spiritual applications of doctrinal truth.[72]

There are three groups listed as "elementary principles" (verses 1-2). They are centered on *salvation* (repentance, faith); *ordinances* (baptisms, the laying on of hands); and *the final state* (resurrection, eternal judgment).

Repentance from dead works—repentance is such a sorrow for sin that the one who sins will seek to turn away from it with all his heart. One cannot remain in a life of sin and disobedience to God, and still honor the Lord. Repentance is a deliberate, willful turning away from sin, and following after God.

Faith toward God—faith is a state of the mind in which the things of God become gloriously certain. The things pertaining to God and salvation cannot always be explained in a logical and scientific way. True saving faith is the kind that results in obedience.

The doctrine of baptisms—may refer to the various

---

[72] Too many in our churches are satisfied with a very shallow understanding of even the basic doctrines of the Christian faith.

kinds of Jewish washings (the Greek word is not the usual word for "baptism"), but is more likely a reference to the variety of Christian baptisms—the baptism of fire, the baptism of the Holy Spirit, and baptism with water.[73]

Laying on of hands—was an apostolic practice, and is a rite associated with healing, baptism, and conveying the responsibilities of a church office (Acts 19:5-6; James 5:14; 1 Timothy 4:14). It is a symbol of the coming of the Holy Spirit in new power to help meet a task at hand.[74]

Resurrection of the dead—sometimes refers to the miraculous raisings of the dead back to earthly life, as in 2 Kings 4:18-37; generally it speaks of a future time when the dead will be raised and will give an account to God.

Eternal judgment—the New Testament teaches that Christ is the Judge; Calvary is the place where the believer's sins have been judged; eternal separation from God is the judgment upon unbelievers.

The writer does not mean that the simpler teachings are to be forgotten or denied or neglected. His point is that attention is not to be limited to them. We learn the alphabet in order to be able to read, but we go on from there.

Christians must not neglect and forget the elementary doctrines of the faith. The writer of Hebrews says that the Lord wants His people *to go on* to a greater level of maturity (verse 3). The writer himself is committed to lead on in that direction "if God permits"—that is, if death or the Lord's coming does not prevent that goal from happening.

---

[73] Mennonite writer, Daniel Kauffman, says: "As a religious ceremony performed by man we have but one kind of baptism, namely, water baptism, but the Bible speaks of three other kinds"—and then he names Spirit baptism, baptism with fire, and baptism of suffering (*Doctrines of the Bible*, page 384).

[74] For more on the laying on of hands, see page 57 in *New Testament Beliefs and Practices: A Brethren Understanding*, Harold S. Martin, and also pages 126-130 in *Studies in Doctrine and Devotion*, by Kurtz, Blough, and Ellis.

3. There Is No Second Beginning (6:4-8)

Some have feared that because they were guilty of some serious disobedience or neglect, perhaps even long continued—that they might be unable to repent and therefore will be condemned forever. It is important to be reminded that temporary backsliding is very different from a deliberate renunciation of Christ.

(6:4-6) For it is impossible for those who were once enlightened, and have tasted the heavenly gift, and have become partakers of the Holy Spirit, and have tasted the good word of God and the powers of the age to come, if they fall away, to renew them again to repentance, since they crucify again for themselves the Son of God, and put Him to an open shame.

This is one of the very difficult passages in the Bible to interpret. Hundreds of pages have been written by Bible students, seeking to blunt the cutting edge of the passage, by diluting the thrust of the words.[75] The warning is very strong; the writer tells of some who have fallen away from their experiences of divine grace, instead of going on to maturity as he had urged in verses 1-3.[76]

Verses 4 and 5 describe the condition of those who fell away. They were *"once enlightened"*—that is, they were

---

[75]   Some writers say that the word *"impossible"* (verse 4a) should be translated *"difficult,"* but Hebrews 6:18 ("it is impossible for God to lie"), and Hebrews 10:4 ("it is not possible that the blood of bulls and goats can take away sin") must obviously be interpreted in a very literal way. "Impossible" clearly means "it cannot happen." The writer of Hebrews speaks of those who of their own stubborn volition have set themselves against Christ. They have abandoned His way and despised His truth and spurned His work on the cross.

[76]   The English reformer, John Wesley, says, "The apostle here describes the case of those who have cast away both the power and the form of godliness; who have lost both their faith, hope, and love (Hebrews 6:10), and [did] that willfully (Hebrews 10:26). Of these willful, total apostates he declares it is impossible to renew them again to repentance, though they were renewed once" (*The Classic Bible Commentary, Owen Collins,* editor, page 1449).

transferred out of the condition of darkness into the light of the gospel[77] and into fellowship with Jesus Christ.

They also *"tasted the heavenly gift"*—that is, they not merely *sampled* the heavenly gift,[78] but the word "taste" (Greek, *geuomai*) means "to experience." The word "taste" is a many-faceted word; readers should note that exactly the same word is used in Hebrews 2:9, where the author applies the word "taste" to the death of Jesus, saying that Jesus tasted death for every person. If Jesus *actually experienced* death on the cross, then those who "tasted the heavenly gift" *actually experienced*[79] the gift of new life in Christ.

They had *"become partakers of the Holy Spirit"*—that is, they shared a partnership with the Holy Spirit, and were aware of the indwelling of the Holy Spirit.

They *"tasted the good word of God"*—that is, they experienced the sweet testimony of God's grace, instead of the condemnation and severity of the Old Testament law, as they became more familiar with the Word of God.

They *"tasted...the powers of the age to come"*—which means that they were made familiar with the supernatural events that mark the present age (the power that transforms individuals into peace-loving men and women of God), and

---

[77] Some say they only had light, not life. They tasted, but did not receive. The Greek word translated "enlightened" (*photidzo*) is also translated "bring to light" or "illuminate" or "make to see." J. B. Smith says the same word is used in Luke 11:36; Ephesians 3:9; 2 Timothy 1:10; 1 Corinthians 4:5; Hebrews 10:32, etc. (*Greek-English Concordance*, page 370).

[78] The heavenly "gift" likely refers to Jesus, who identified Himself as "the gift of God" when He talked to the woman at the well (John 4:10), or it may refer to the Holy Spirit who is declared to be a "gift" in Acts 2:38.

[79] Compare the use of the word "taste" in passages like Matthew 16:28, Luke 14:24, Hebrews 2:9, and 1 Peter 2:3. J. C. Macaulay says that *"to argue that 'tasting' of the heavenly gift is something less than 'receiving' it, would require our paring down Christ's 'tasting death for every man' to an experience short of actual death" (Hebrews 2:9).* See *Commentary on Hebrews*, page 79.

of the future age (the power manifested when Jesus returns, as described in 2 Thessalonians 1:7-9).

After describing a number of the early experiences some persons have had, the writer continues by relating what may happen to those who become careless in their Christian life. If such persons *"fall away"* (verse 6), it is impossible to restore them again to repentance.

The writer of Hebrews has repeatedly warned that apostasy can occur (3:12-13; 4:1, 11). He speaks here about apostasy, *falling away* (verse 6), not "falling into sin." For example, *Judas fell away from Jesus* and never returned to Him (Acts 1:15-18). *Peter fell into sin* but soon afterward saw Jesus and repented with tears (Matthew 26:69-75). Judas was involved in *apostasy*; Peter was guilty of *backsliding*. Apostasy and backsliding must not be confused.[80]

Apostasy is a gradual process; it does not take place with suddenness. It is marked by a diminished devotion that begins with unbelief, and progresses to disobedience and a deliberate turning away from the Lord.[81] Apostasy involves more than the backsliding of a feeble Christian who has been tripped up by Satan in an unguarded moment.

The statement *"It is impossible...if they fall away, to renew them again to repentance"* (verse 4a, 6a), means that

---

[80] Neglecting salvation is a dangerous step. Guy Duty comments: "Thousands today who live and persist in [various] unlawful indulgences—have an unshakeable belief that they are eternally predestinated for salvation. They worship the money-god, the pleasure-god, the sex-god, and believe that God has made special provision for them so that they can never be lost. Satan has no greater deception [than this]" (*If Ye Continue*, page 120).

[81] Some embrace the faith of the Lord Jesus and His work on the cross, but with the passing of time, they begin to waver. Instead of pressing on, they gradually lose ground, and eventually defiantly renounce Christ and the power of His cleansing blood. They mock and jeer at His ability to save. Such persons crucify "again" for themselves the Son of God (verse 6), and by this indicate that they have arrived at a state of heart where they no longer even want to repent.

there are some[82] who have been transferred out of the kingdom of darkness into the light of the gospel, but who now have openly disowned the Lord Jesus. It is impossible to renew them again because they have a constant attitude of hostility toward Christ Jesus.[83] Their contempt for Him is a fixed persuasion within their hearts.

The passage in Hebrews 6 alludes to *falling away*, a deliberate renunciation of Christ as the only Savior. The reference is not to *a stumbling* in the way, but to *a departing* from it. The text does not imply that believers lose salvation every time they trip and fall into sin, and then regain salvation again when they repent. Many Christians who falter along the way will quickly repent and receive God's forgiveness. Bible teachers should not declare that people lose salvation every time they fail to live up to God's standard. The warning here is for those who rail on Christ and ridicule Him,[84] and behave much like that first hostile crowd who repeatedly shouted, "Crucify Him!"

Many local church leaders are deeply aware of people in their congregations who have begun the Christian life

---

[82] It is my conviction that very few persons decide to disown the Lord Jesus when they have once received Christ as their Savior, and realize the great promises and blessings that accompany salvation; nevertheless, there is the possibility that apostasy *can* occur. The words "to *renew them again* to repentance" (verse 6) state clearly that they were once renewed.

[83] God has pledged to pardon every person who truly repents. However, there are some persons who arrive at a state of heart in which repentance is impossible. Thomas Lea says, "It is not impossible because God is not willing to bring them to repentance, but it is impossible because the person is so hardened he will not repent" (*Holman New Testament Commentary: Hebrews*, page 111).

[84] "One of the most sublime truths of the New Testament…is God's self limitation. He will not transgress or abuse human freedom. The same God who will not save a man against his will, will not keep a man saved against his will…As long as a soul desires and wills to love and serve God, he is secure, but when he chooses to return to the slavery of sin God will respect that decision" (R. E. Howard, *Beacon Bible Commentary, Volume 9, Galatians—Philemon*, page 84).

with great promise and many evidences of having had a new birth experience, but since have turned their backs on Christ and now seem plainly embarrassed about their Christian commitment and the vows they made at the time of baptism. Most Christians know of some people who were once warm hearted fellow believers, but who now have deliberately rejected their loyalty to Jesus Christ.

It is helpful to notice again that the text says that *"it is impossible...if they fall away, to renew them again to repentance"* (verses 4a, 6a). For the ordinary backslider, repentance and restoration is a possibility, but when a person chooses a constant attitude of hostility toward Jesus Christ, repentance is impossible. But as long as individuals feel that they *need* to repent, and they *want* to repent—they have not gone too far.

(6:7-8) For the earth which drinks in the rain that often comes upon it, and bears herbs useful for those by whom it is cultivated, receives blessing from God; but if it bears thorns and briars, it is rejected and near to being cursed, whose end is to be burned.

The writer of Hebrews now brings the strong warning to a close by using a parable from agricultural life.

The illustration describes two kinds of land. Both types of land, the good and the bad (symbols of the genuine and the apostate), have received the refreshing rain that often falls on it. The true Christian is like soil that responds to the rain from heaven and produces useful vegetation, therefore receiving additional blessing from God (verse 7).

The other land also has received the refreshing rains, but it bears useless thorns and thistles. It is rejected and abandoned as worthless land, and in the end the useless weeds are burned. What a sad ending. Those who take the road to apostasy are like the land that is well watered, but bears nothing useful and is destined to burn (verse 8).

4. Exhortation to Perseverance (6:9-12)

In contrast to those who have withdrawn and retracted their allegiance to the Christian faith, the writer of Hebrews is convinced that his readers were not in that class.

(6:9-12) But, beloved, we are confident of better things concerning you, yes, things that accompany salvation, though we speak in this manner. For God is not unjust to forget your work and labor of love which you have shown toward His name, in that you have ministered to the saints, and do minister. And we desire that each one of you show the same diligence to the full assurance of hope until the end, that you do not become sluggish, but imitate those who through faith and patience inherit the promises.

In light of the warning given in verses 4-8, the writer gives some words of encouragement when he says, "We are confident of better things concerning you" (verse 9). His optimism is based on the faithfulness of God, *who will not forget* loyal service and labors of *love* in His kingdom (verse 10).[85] These words of encouragement should be an incentive for Christians to continue diligently serving the Lord until the very end of life's journey.

Thomas Lea (in the *Holman* commentary) tells about Vladimir Bojev, who in 1979 was "a tough, hard-drinking Russian unbeliever." Bojev barged into a Christian service one Lord's Day and threatened to kill the people who were in the audience. But one of the Christians in that assembly suggested that they gather around Bojev and pray for him. Bojev was visibly moved by the evidence of their concern

---

[85] When the faithful disciple serves the needs of others around him, God sees it. God notices it, and He is not unrighteous to forget. Our labor for God is not in vain. What an encouragement that should be to our hearts! God's people must never grow weary in well doing, for in due season we shall reap (Galatians 6:9).

and love for him. He came back to the services, later received Christ as his Savior, and married a girl from the church. Bojev said, "Their love won me to Christ and I was converted." He eventually became pastor of another church some 200 miles southwest of Moscow.

Just as God remembers loyal service rendered to Him and His people (verse 10), so Christians are not to be sluggish (verse 12), but intensely earnest about imitating those who through faith *persevered in hope* to the end (verse 11).

Christians are to throw off spiritual laziness and lay hold of the hope[86] which is given to believers when they come to faith in Christ. Genuine *hope* is not merely wishful thinking, nor is it a blind desire to have something happen. God has a track-record of faithfulness in the past, and we can count upon His promises, knowing that promises will be fulfilled like He said they would be.

Those whose hope was fixed in Christ, through *faith* and patience inherited God's promises (verse 12). Believers are exhorted to imitate their example of faith[87] in God.

5. God's Promises Are Certain (6:13-20)

This section continues the exposition on hope, a very important concept if Christians are to stay loyal to Christ.

---

[86] One Bible teacher tells of his visit with a native preacher in Nigeria. The black preacher had a brother who was an unconverted tribal chief—a cruel, hard man. The difference between these two brothers *as they were observed talking together* was evident in many ways. The eyes of the tribal chief showed great cruelty; his features were hard and pitiless. The other man (the preacher) had a countenance that showed kindness and calmness. The kindly native preacher was once a man of cruelty like his brother, but now that preacher *had become a child of hope* and even his countenance showed the difference. The word "hope" appears in most of the books of the New Testament.

[87] It is interesting and instructive to note the faith, hope, and charity trilogy in these verses—love (verse 10), hope, (verse 11), and faith (verse 12). The triad of graces is found at a number of places in the Bible.

(6:13-20) For when God made a promise to Abraham, because He could swear by no one greater, He swore by Himself, saying, "Surely blessing I will bless you, and multiplying I will multiply you." And so, after he had patiently endured, he obtained the promise. For men indeed swear by the greater, and an oath for confirmation is for them an end of all dispute. Thus God, determining to show more abundantly to the heirs of promise the immutability of His counsel, confirmed it by an oath, that by two immutable things, in which it is impossible for God to lie, we might have strong consolation, who have fled for refuge to lay hold of the hope set before us. This hope we have as an anchor of the soul, both sure and steadfast, and which enters the Presence behind the veil, where the forerunner has entered for us, even Jesus, having become High Priest forever according to the order of Melchizedek.

Abraham is introduced here (verses 13-15) as an example of perseverance. He endured a long time before Isaac was born. There were times when he feared that the promise God had made in Genesis 15:5-6 (and confirmed in Genesis 17:6-8) might not materialize, but he patiently endured, and in his old age he was given a son (verse 15).

After Abraham's faith stood the severe test of his willingness to offer up Isaac as a sacrifice to the Lord (Genesis 22:16-18), God gave him a further and final confirmation by an oath made to him and given in strong and emphatic terms (Hebrews 6:16-17).

In Genesis 12:2-3, God promised that blessing would come on Abraham and on his descendants. That promise, after many years, was fulfilled in the coming of Jesus Christ, who was of the seed of Abraham (Galatians 3:8,16).

God confirmed His promise by "two immutable things" (verse 18). The two unchangeable facts that supported what God said were *His promise* and *His oath*. An oath is an appeal to a higher power,[88] but there is no power higher than Jehovah God, so He swore by Himself (verse 13).

The writer says that God has reinforced His promise of blessing, and this provides *hope* for believers (verses 18-20). Faith in the work of Jesus (the offspring of Abraham) is a firm basis for the Christian's hope—because His finished work on the cross continues in Heaven (verse 19b), and He will serve as the believer's High Priest *forever* because He is a priest after the order of Melchizedek (verse 20b).

Christian hope[89] teaches us to say, *"For our light affliction, which is but for a moment, is working for us a far more exceeding and eternal weight of glory"* (2 Corinthians 4:17). Christian hope is valid because it is nourished by the promises of God: "Blessed be the…Father of our Lord Jesus Christ, who…has begotten us again *to a living hope* through the resurrection of Jesus Christ from the dead" (1 Peter 1:3). Our eternal destiny does not depend on the shifting sands of

---

[88] God used an *oath* (Genesis 22:16-18), not to reinforce His promise, but to strengthen the faith of Abraham. God condescended to man's way of guaranteeing a promise, by supplying evidence that no one could doubt. Some wonder why God would use an oath, when He prohibits His disciples from oath-taking. No act of God can be sin—no matter how sinful it may be for human beings. God may take the lives of innocent men and women in an earthquake or flood, and not be committing sin; yet the taking of human life would be sin for us. John W. Haley says, "The Jews in that age were in the habit of using vain and frivolous oaths in their ordinary talk. They swore by the temple, by the earth, by heaven, and by their head. So long as they did not use the name of God in those oaths, they did not deem them particularly binding. This practice is alluded to in Matthew 23:16-22" (*Alleged Discrepancies in the Bible*, page 243).

[89] Hope is "desire, with expectancy." The question, "Would you like to make a million dollars next year?" *is desire, but no expectancy.* The question, "Are you going to pay your income tax by April 15? *is expectancy, but perhaps with no desire.* The coming of Jesus to complete our redemption *is desire, with expectancy.* Christian hope is not mere wishful thinking (a blind desire to have something happen), nor is it a mere optimistic temperament (the ability to look at the bright side of everything). Christian hope is a firm conviction that God's promises will indeed materialize.

man's philosophy, but on the sure promises of God.

The eternal work of Jesus as High Priest is likened to *an anchor*, which is a heavy object[90] on a ship. It is designed to be cast overboard, sinking deep into the sea, in order to hold the vessel in a particular place. Just so, the strong and trustworthy promises of God serve as an anchor to calm our fears in the storms of life. In the closing verses of Hebrews 6, we are encouraged to cultivate the virtue of hope, and to make it one of the priorities in our spiritual lives.

As we face the mysteries and uncertainties of life, what can we trust? Whom can we believe? What is there to hold on to in the midst of storms that toss our ships from side to side? It is *the hope* that has been set before us.

Priscilla Owens expresses the truth in a beautiful hymn:
"We have an anchor that keeps the soul,
Steadfast and sure while the billows roll;
Fastened to the Rock which cannot move,
Grounded firm and deep in the Savior's love."

Our *hope* is fixed on Jesus,[91] the "spiritual Rock" who sustains His people, and who has now entered the presence of God "behind the veil" (verse 19)[92] to serve as a Mediator forever for those who have embraced Him as Savior—and thus *our hope* lies unseen in the highest heaven.

---

[90]   Near the Peabody Maritime Museum in Salem, Massachusetts, visitors can see an old anchor that weighs 4,004 pounds. It was once used to secure a ship.
[91]   In Elwood Mote's hymn entitled "The Solid Rock," one of the stanzas says, *"His oath, His covenant, His blood—support me in the whelming flood. When all around my soul gives way, He then is all my hope and stay."*
[92]   The "Presence behind the veil" is a figure drawn from the Jewish Temple where the high priest went behind the curtain in the Holy of Holies on the Day of Atonement to sprinkle the blood of atonement on the Mercy Seat (the lid of the Ark of the covenant). God had promised to be there. Now, in the present age, Jesus has entered into Heaven itself, not with the blood of bulls and goats, but with His own blood to continually be an Advocate for our cause.

Chapter 6

CHRIST IS SUPERIOR IN HIS PRIESTLY ORDER
Hebrews 7:1-28

For many Christians, the story of the life of Christ seems to end with His resurrection and ascension. They may have a vague idea about the return of Christ some day, but often fail to grasp all that Christ is doing *now*.

Christians with an Anabaptist background do not use the word "priest" very often; yet, one of the most important ministries of Jesus on our behalf is that of functioning as our High Priest, interceding for us before the heavenly Father.

In Hebrews 7, the reader is taken back to the subject of Christ's function as a High Priest after the rank of Melchizedek, a truth which the writer had begun to discuss in Hebrews 4:14—5:10.[93] He continues to proclaim the truth that Christ's priesthood was like that of Melchizedek rather than like that of Aaron.[94] This part of the letter is one which readers sometimes find difficult to follow.

1. The History of Melchizedek (7:1-3)

Melchizedek was a historical person. His superiority to Abraham is shown in that Abraham paid tithes to him.

(7:1-3) For this Melchizedek, king of Salem, priest of the Most High God, who met Abraham returning from the slaughter of the kings and blessed him, to whom also Abraham gave a tenth part of all, first being translated "king of righteousness," and then also king of Salem, meaning "king of peace," without father, without mother, without genealogy,

---

[93] It will be helpful to read pages 57-68 again in this commentary.
[94] Raymond Brown observes, "It is not Jesus who resembles Melchizedek, but Melchizedek who resembles the Lord Jesus" (*Christ Above All*, page 129).

having neither beginning of days nor end of life, but made like the Son of God, remains a priest continually.

The story of Melchizedek's meeting Abraham is a short account found in Genesis 14:18-20. Abraham had gone to rescue his nephew Lot from the armies of a confederation of kings who had gone against the king of Sodom and his allies. Upon returning home, Abraham was met on the way by "Melchizedek, king of Salem, priest of the Most High God" (verse 1). Melchizedek "blessed" Abraham, and Abraham gave tithes to Melchizedek (verse 2).

Melchizedek was a Canaanite *king* (a ruler over the people), and a *priest* (an intercessor with God for the people). Melchizedek believed in the living God, and blessed Abraham in the name of "God Most High" (Genesis 14:19). Evidently there was a group of people who lived in ancient Jerusalem, who had known the true Creator-God. Melchizedek was their king-priest. His lack of genealogy (verse 3) *does not mean* that Melchizedek was a supernatural being who had no parents, or that he was born and did not die, but that the Scriptures have no record of these events.[95]

The words, "having neither beginning of days nor end of life" (verse 3), mean, that as far as the record goes, Melchizedek's span of life is unknown to us. And we know that Jesus is the eternal God, and therefore He never had a beginning nor will He ever cease to exist. So Melchizedek symbolically (in terms of life-span) becomes a person from early Israelite history who prefigures Christ.

---

[95] Some believe that Melchizedek actually *was Christ* appearing to Abraham in human form (a Christophany); others believe that Melchizedek was a human being, but that there is no record of who Melchizedek's parents were, or of his birth and death. F. B. Meyer held the first view and says that the Genesis account of the priesthood of Melchizedek is so remarkable that it seems "as though the appearance of Melchizedek to Abraham was one of the Christophanies of the Old Testament" (*An Exposition of the Whole Bible*, page 515).

Both Christ and Melchizedek were men (Hebrews 7:4; 1 Timothy 2:5). Both were "king-priests" (Genesis 14:18; Zechariah 6:12-13). Both were appointed by God (Hebrews 7:21). Both were promoting "righteousness" and "peace" (Isaiah 11:1-9; Hebrews 7:1-2). In Hebrews 7, Jesus Christ is likened to the rank of Melchizedek.

2. The Greatness of Melchizedek (7:4-10)

To identify Melchizedek *with certainty* is really a vain pursuit. As far as the record is concerned, we know nothing about his origin. He simply came on the scene, fulfilled his ministry, and departed.

(7:4-10) Now consider how great this man was, to whom even the patriarch Abraham gave a tenth of the spoils. And indeed those who are of the sons of Levi, who receive the priesthood, have a commandment to receive tithes from the people according to the law, that is, from their brethren, though they have come from the loins of Abraham; but he whose genealogy is not derived from them received tithes from Abraham and blessed him who had the promises. Now beyond all contradiction the lesser is blessed by the better. Here mortal men receive tithes, but there he receives them, of whom it is witnessed that he lives. Even Levi, who receives tithes, paid tithes through Abraham, so to speak, for he was still in the loins of his father when Melchizedek met him.

No one disputed the greatness of *Abraham*. Jews considered him as the father of Israel; Christians saw him as the father of all who believe (Romans 4:11), but in verses 4-10, the greatness of *Melchizedek* is shown in several ways.[96]

First: Melchizedek is seen as superior to Levi, in that Levi's great grandfather (Abraham) *paid tithes* to Mel-

---

[96] By using the story concerning Melchizedek, the discussion of the priesthood of Christ is resumed. The reference to Christ's priesthood was begun in 4:14.

chizedek (Hebrews 7:2,6). Jesus could not have been a Levitical priest because He was born of the tribe of Judah, not of Levi (Hebrews 7:14). Thus Jesus must be associated with another order of priests—that of Melchizedek.

Second: Melchizedek *placed a blessing* upon the highly respected man Abraham. It is generally agreed that the person who has the power to bless is always greater than the person he blesses (verse 7).

Third: The word "here" (verse 8a) refers to the Levitical priests; the word "there" refers to Melchizedek and his priesthood. It also refers to Christ who is a Priest after the rank of Melchizedek, who as far as the record goes, lives on.

Fourth: We learn that Levitical priests, descendants of Aaron, paid tithes to Melchizedek in the person of their ancestor Abraham (verses 9-10). The proof that the Melchizedek priesthood (and therefore Christ's priesthood) is superior to the (Levitical) priesthood, is that Levi's great grandfather (Abraham) paid tithes to Melchizedek—and therefore Levi,[97] before he was born, was involved in that transaction (verse 9).

These have been examples designed to demonstrate ways by which the priesthood of Melchizedek ranks far above the Levitical priesthood. Christ is a Priest after the order of Melchizedek.

3. Limitations of the Levitical Priesthood (7:11-14)

The Mosaic Law and the Levitical priesthood could not give people "perfection"—that is, a complete reconciliation with God. The word "perfection" (*teleosis*) speaks here of

---

[97]   It was Abraham who paid the tithes to Melchizedek (Genesis 14:20), but Levi (the great-grandson of Abraham) *also paid tithes* to Melchizedek, because he was physically "in the loins of [Abraham]." So, it was *as if* Levi and all his tribe paid tithes to this priest-king.

complete communion with God. This is another proof that Christ is superior to the Levitical priests.

(7:11-14) Therefore, if perfection were through the Levitical priesthood (for under it the people received the law), what further need was there that another priest should rise according to the order of Melchizedek, and not be called according to the order of Aaron? For the priesthood being changed, of necessity there is also a change of the law. For He of whom these things are spoken belongs to another tribe, from which no man has officiated at the altar. For it is evident that our Lord arose from Judah, of which tribe Moses spoke nothing concerning priesthood.

The old Jewish order of priesthood is set aside because of its weakness and imperfection. The saving intercessory work of Christ provides a better hope, and is the only means by which sinful humans can draw near to God.

The writer does not belittle Moses and Aaron, but he shows how far superior Christ is to them. Levitical priests were appointed to serve because of their ancestry as sons of Aaron (Exodus 28:1; Leviticus 8-9). They themselves were sinners and eventually died (7:23-25). Jesus, by way of contrast, was from the tribe of Judah, and served on the basis of power flowing from a life that would never end.

4. Jesus' Priesthood is a Spiritual Priesthood (7:15-19)

Levitical priests were appointed priests because they were the sons of certain parents. Their appointment did not necessarily depend on their spiritual qualifications.

(7:15-19) And it is yet far more evident if, in the likeness of Melchizedek, there arises another priest who has come, not according to the law of a fleshly commandment, but according to the power of an endless life. For He testifies: "You are a priest forever according to the order of Melchizedek." For on the one hand there is an annulling of the former command-

ment because of its weakness and unprofitableness, for the law made nothing perfect; on the other hand, there is the bringing in of a better hope, through which we draw near to God.

The Mosaic Law said that the priests were to be the offspring of Aaron, who was from the tribe of Levi. Levitical priests served because they were Aaron's descendants. Their appointment to the priesthood did not depend upon their spiritual qualifications or their desire to serve. They did their duty because the law said that the Levites from the family of Aaron shall be priests (verse 16).

Jesus served as a priest because of an inner delight to do the Father's will. Jesus lives on eternally and thus the order of Melchizedek was typical of His priesthood (verse 17).

These verses picture the Mosaic Law as an inadequate instrument (verse 18). It provided a proper moral standard, but it did not provide the spiritual stamina to reach that standard and live by it. The "better hope" (verse 19) refers to the fact that the priesthood of Jesus *effects full removal* of sin, and *provides a new way of access* to God.

5. Jesus' Priesthood is an Unchangeable Priesthood (7:20-22)

The priests of Aaron's line were inaugurated without oaths, but Christ was appointed priest with a solemn oath.

(7:20-22) And inasmuch as He was not made priest without an oath (for they have become priests without an oath, but He with an oath by Him who said to Him: "The LORD has sworn and will not relent, 'You are a priest forever according to the order of Melchizedek'"), by so much more Jesus has become a surety of a better covenant.

The "they" (verse 21) refers to the Levitical priests under the old covenant who were appointed because they were to be offspring of Aaron. The "He" refers to Jesus who was declared a Priest after the rank of Melchizedek. The priesthood of Jesus was determined by a declaration of God (verse 17), which was further confirmed by an oath (verse 20). An oath was considered to be solemnly binding; it served to settle a matter beyond further dispute. God used an oath, not because He needed to reinforce His word, but to strengthen the faith of His floundering people.

The earthly high priest had to atone for his own sins, and eventually died. Jesus lives forever. The word "surety" (*egguos*) appears only here in the New Testament (verse 22), and it introduces a better[98] "covenant." This is the first time the word "covenant" is used in the book of Hebrews, but it will be used frequently hereafter.

6. Jesus' Priesthood is an Uninterrupted Priesthood (7:23-25)

In the Levitical priesthood, there were interruptions and changes due to death of the priests, but in contrast, Christ lives forever, and His priesthood is never interrupted.

(7:23-25) Also there were many priests, because they were prevented by death from continuing. But He, because He continues forever, has an unchangeable priesthood. Therefore He is also able to save to the uttermost those who come to God through Him, since He always lives to make intercession for them.

The Levitical priests eventually died because they were human (verse 23). No matter how dedicated Levitical priests may have been, death put an abrupt end to their ministry. By way of contrast, Jesus is present everywhere, but there is a sense in which He is in heaven mediating in behalf of believers as they approach God through Him. And since He lives forever, His priesthood is never interrupted.

---

[98]   Jesus, as a High Priest after the order of Melchizedek, will serve forever. That will be "better"—which is a key word in the book of Hebrews. Christ is better than the angels (1:4); He brought in a better hope (7:19); He is Mediator of a better covenant (8:6); the faithful desire a better country (11:16); etc.

The "unchangeable priesthood" (verse 24) is a clear fact because Jesus Christ never changes. He is the same yesterday, today, and forever. Also, the gospel never changes; it is still the power of God unto salvation. The promises of God never change; they are fixed, and will prove reliable forever.

Christ is able to save "to the uttermost" (verse 25), meaning that He can save completely and eternally, no matter how deeply into sin a person may have gone.[99] The writer of Hebrews has much to say about Christ's redemptive work on the cross *in the past*, but he also emphasizes Christ's *present work* for His people. Christ's *saving* ministry has been accomplished, but now He supports believers through His ministry of intercession.

7. Jesus' Priesthood is a Suitable Priesthood (7:26-28)

The priesthood of Jesus is necessary and appropriate for human beings since we are sinful and frail and dependent. We must have a Savior, Mediator, and High Priest in whom we can have perfect confidence.

(7:26-28) For such a High Priest was fitting for us, who is holy, harmless, undefiled, separate from sinners, and has become higher than the heavens; who does not need daily, as those high priests, to offer up sacrifices, first for His own sins and then for the people's, for this He did once for all when He offered up Himself. For the law appoints as high priests men who have weakness, but the word of the oath, which came

---

[99]   John MacArthur says, "Publicans, prostitutes, thieves, and beggars all found in Christ a Savior who gave them abundant and everlasting life in exchange for the remnants of their squandered earthly existence. He came to seek and save the lost, and He loved plucking them as brands from the fire. No one, no matter how dissipated by sin, was beyond the reach of His redemptive power. He did what no one else could do for them. He cast legions of stubborn evil spirits out of the demon-possessed (Luke 8:26-35), and He touched and made whole the ravaged bodies of lepers (Matthew 8:1-3). He gravitated to such people, and they in turn were drawn to Him for salvation" (*The Gospel According to Jesus*, page 149).

**after the law, appoints the Son who has been perfected for-
ever.**

All human beings falter along the journey of life, and so
we need a Mediator—someone who can bring about reconciliation between us and God.

Death ended the priestly functions of the Levites, but
Christ *through His resurrection* has an unending priesthood
(verse 24). Since *there is no break* in the ongoing function of
His priesthood, His order is necessarily better.

Our High Priest (Jesus Christ) is divinely perfect. Since
this is so, believers must turn from all self-confidence, all
human ceremonies, all other mediators—and draw near to
God through Him. For those who embrace the Lord Jesus,
His death cancels their condemnation, and His life guarantees their access into the very presence of God.

Jesus lived a *holy* life (verse 26), has always been entirely without sin. His life was dedicated to the service of
God and was pleasing to the heavenly Father.

Christ's life was *harmless* (Greek, *akakos*), meaning
"free from malice and craft." His life was *undefiled* (Greek,
amiantos), meaning "free from that which is deformed or
debased by sin" (verse 26). He lived a *separated* life, committed to doing the will of God and not inclined to com-
promise with sinners.

The Old Testament priesthood was weak, imperfect,
and could not save. The Mosaic Law appointed men as high
priests. By way of contrast, Christ's priesthood is perfect and
it takes away sin. His priesthood meets our needs. Christ,
who is holy, innocent, and unstained, can deal with sin and
stand for us in the presence of God.

The early readers of Hebrews were primarily Israelites
who had embraced the Christian faith. The author of the
book tried to make every argument in the letter crystal clear,

and so he emphasized his points by repeating them. Even though his readers were true believers in Christ, they were perplexed by this major change in the priesthood.

From early times, the Israelites accepted God's revelation through Moses. The Levitical priesthood, by which they attained access with God was clearly presented in the law. The priests were the sons of Aaron (Leviticus 21:1); their task was to officiate at worship by offering various offerings on behalf of the nation, and by leading the people to confess their sins (Leviticus 4:20, 26, 31). The high priest was the chief among the priests.

We can understand the reluctance of the Christians in New Testament times (many of whom were Jewish in background), to accept this new revelation about a rather mysterious person named Melchizedek. Some were slow to accept the high priesthood of Jesus, which functioned in the rank of Melchizedek instead of in the rank of Aaron who was one of their own relatives (from the tribe of Levi).

Today, New Testament Christians tend to emphasize *the finished work* of Christ on the cross, but Hebrews 7 reminds us also about *the continuing and ongoing work* of Christ. When we falter along the path in our earthly journey, He steps forward, and as our Attorney, pleads our case before the Father (1 John 2:1).

We have seen the *Superior Person of Christ* in the first major section of Hebrews. Christ is superior to the prophets (1:1-3); He is superior to the angels (1:4—2:18); He is superior to Moses and Aaron, and to the human priests from the tribe of Levi (3:1—7:28). We will discover in the second major section of the book of Hebrews, an emphasis on the *Superior Provisions of Calvary* (8:1—10:18).

Part II
THE SUPERIOR PROVISIONS OF CALVARY
Hebrews 8:1—10:18

Chapter 7

OPERATION OF THE FIRST COVENANT
Hebrews 8:1—9:10

In Hebrews 8, a new line of argument appears. The writer already introduced the reader to *the high priest* and his offering of sacrifices. He explained that Christ had made a perfect sacrifice and has ascended into the heavens.

In these chapters, a new element is introduced into his explanation; Jesus was like Melchizedek (with no predecessors or successors), *but He also* established a new and better covenant with mankind.[100] We will learn that in the new agreement Christ's sacrifice of Himself *replaces* the sacrifice of bulls and goats which were offered in Old Testament times (9:1—10:18).

1. Christ is the Minister of a Better Covenant (8:1-13)

In Jesus believers have a High Priest who has offered a dynamic sacrifice for sin. In contrast with the Levitical priests, Jesus provided a more adequate sacrifice and made possible *a better covenant* between the sinner and God.

The idea of a covenant is a very significant concept, especially for the Jews. A "covenant" is an agreement between two people or two groups that involves promises on the part of each to the other.

---

[100] The writer contrasts two covenants—the old, or first covenant, and the new, or second covenant. The old covenant was the one made between God and Israel at Sinai (verse 9). The new covenant is the one between God and His people, made on the basis of the death of Jesus (verses 8, 10-12). The new covenant is said to apply to "the house of Israel" (verse 10a), but the promise is for all of God's people, both Jews and Gentiles. Galatians 3:29 says, *"And if you are Christ's, then you are Abraham's seed, and heirs according to the promise."*

(8:1-5) Now this is the main point of the things we are saying: We have such a High Priest, who is seated at the right hand of the throne of the Majesty in the heavens, a Minister of the sanctuary and of the true tabernacle which the Lord erected, and not man. For every high priest is appointed to offer both gifts and sacrifices. Therefore it is necessary that this One also have something to offer. For if He were on earth, He would not be a priest, since there are priests who offer the gifts according to the law; who serve the copy and shadow of the heavenly things, as Moses was divinely instructed when he was about to make the tabernacle. For He said, "See that you make all things according to the pattern shown you on the mountain."

The summary of what was described in Hebrews 7 is stated here at the beginning of Hebrews 8. We have in this age a High Priest who has taken His seat at the right hand of "the Majesty in the heavens" (verse 1).[101] To be "seated" was a mark of honor[102] and authority, and "the Majesty in the heavens" is another term for the true and living God.

Jesus serves "in the true tabernacle" (verse 2), a reference to the heavenly realm where He is seated at the right hand of God serving as a "Minister of the sanctuary"—in the true place of worship. The word "minister" (Greek, *leitourgos*) denotes *the activity* of the priest.[103] The supreme function of any priest is to open the way to God for sinful

---

[101] Otho Winger, in his *History and Doctrines of the Church of the Brethren*, wrote in 1920, that Brethren believe that Jesus "ascended on high (Acts 1:9), and is now at the right hand of the Father (Hebrews 8:1)."

[102] Jesus is the exalted Lord, the Son of God. Many today attempt to reduce His stature, and think of Him in terms of their idea of who He ought to be. The news writer in *U. S. News and World Report* magazine, commenting on Dan Brown's *DaVinci Code*, says that Brown claims "the early Christians thought of Jesus as a great and powerful man, but a man nonetheless" (page 47, May 22, 2006).

[103] In heaven Jesus presents His wounds and pleads the efficacy of the work He accomplished on the cross at Calvary in behalf of sinful human beings. Jesus has secured forgiveness for those who claim Him as Savior and Lord.

human beings. The priest *builds the bridge* across which men and women can go into the very presence of God.

The high priest was to "offer both gifts and sacrifices" (verse 3). When people brought their meal offerings (gifts) and animals for sacrifices, the priests offered them to God for the sins of the people. The author of Hebrews does not call Jesus by name (verse 3b). He simply says "this One" will have "something" to offer. What the "something" consists of is not stated *until Hebrews 9:14* where the offering is stated to be "the blood of Christ, who through the eternal Spirit offered Himself without spot to God."

Jesus did not belong to the tribe of Levi and therefore He did not qualify as an earthly priest to serve at the altar. The law (verse 4) required that the priests must be from the family of Aaron, who was from the tribe of Levi.[104] Instead, Jesus serves in the true tabernacle, in the presence of God. He offers *Himself* as a gift and sacrifice.

God had provided exact instructions about the details of the tabernacle (verse 5b). If God was concerned about the small details of the earthly tabernacle, surely the heavenly sanctuary was even more glorious. The priests of Old Testament times ministered in an earthly tabernacle which was only *a copy* of the heavenly one (verse 5a), and was limited by time and space. The sacrifices offered in the earthly tent were only *shadows* of the sacrifice which Jesus made. The priesthood of Jesus is superior because He ministers in the heavenly sanctuary.

Because of the ministry of Jesus in our behalf, we may take heart in walking through the journey of life. Those who feel *crushed* and *dejected* and *broken* must remember that

---

[104] The priests were the offspring of Aaron, the great-grandson of Levi, and the first high priest of the Hebrew nation. The Levites were helpers to the priests, with special responsibilities toward attending to the needs of the tabernacle.

Jesus offered His blood for us, and now He is praying for us and pleading our cause before the heavenly Father. Our names are enrolled in heaven, and we are constantly being remembered before the throne of God. Our confidence is rooted in what God's Son has done for us.

The old covenant of the law centered on external ceremonies. Those who choose to accept Christ as Savior, by way of contrast, find that they are given new inward desires to love and serve God (verse 10).

Under the *new covenant*, Christ is at the right hand of the Father, continually pleading our case (Hebrews 8:1-2). Under the *old covenant* the Levitical priests stood for only a short time in the Most Holy Place of the Jewish tabernacle—on just one day of a year.

The Old Testament priest stood before *a symbol* of God's presence (the Mercy Seat on the Ark of the Covenant), whereas Jesus is seated *actually* before God himself.

(8:6-9) But now He has obtained a more excellent ministry, inasmuch as He is also Mediator of a better covenant, which was established on better promises. For if that first covenant had been faultless, then no place would have been sought for a second. Because finding fault with them, He says: "Behold, the days are coming, says the LORD, when I will make a new covenant with the house of Israel and with the house of Judah—not according to the covenant that I made with their fathers in the day when I took them by the hand to lead them out of the land of Egypt; because they did not continue in My covenant, and I disregarded them, says the LORD."

The ministry of Jesus is more effective in its service than that of the Levitical priests in Old Testament times, because God has established Jesus' ministry on better promises (verse 6). Those better promises are explained in verses 10-12 of Hebrews 8.

The *failure* of the first covenant required the instituting of a second (or new) covenant (verse 7).[105] The writer of the letter to the Hebrews then once again quotes a lengthy passage from the Old Testament (verses 8-12). The quote this time is from Jeremiah 31:31-34.

Verse 8 begins the quotation from Jeremiah 31 to explain the new covenant which God had begun. The new agreement was made with the people of Israel and Judah. The text clearly identifies Jeremiah's words as *God's* word. Jeremiah spoke these words at the time when God was restoring the Israelites after the Babylonian Captivity. The new covenant was only established, and the promise fulfilled, centuries later at the time when Jesus the Messiah came to earth during His first Advent.

Verse 9 contrasts the old agreement with the new, by describing the circumstances under which the old agreement was given. The old covenant was initiated when God took the Israelites by the hand to lead them out of the land of Egypt at the time of the Exodus.

In that covenant, God gave Israel His law at Sinai and expected them to obey, but they disregarded God's commands. Since Israel *"did not continue in My covenant...I disregarded them, says the Lord"* (verse 9b).

In the concluding verses of Hebrews 8 the reader is given a description of the new covenant.

(8:10-13) "For this is the covenant that I will make with the house of Israel after those days, says the LORD: I will put My laws in their mind and write them on their hearts; and I will be their God, and they shall be My people. None of them

---

[105] The failure of the first covenant given at Sinai does not suggest that the law itself had flaws, but that the minds of sinful people were corrupt, and they lacked the power to obey the law (Romans 7:7-12). Therefore God introduced a new covenant which is first described in Jeremiah 31.

shall teach his neighbor, and none his brother, saying, 'Know the LORD,' for all shall know Me, from the least of them to the greatest of them. For I will be merciful to their unrighteousness, and their sins and their lawless deeds I will remember no more." In that He says, "A new covenant," He has made the first obsolete. Now what is becoming obsolete and growing old is ready to vanish away.

Many cannot explain the heart of the Christian message. They think Christianity is observing external practices such as going to church, being a moral person, and being nice. These things are important, but under the new covenant God's laws are written in the hearts of true Christians.

The new covenant has a spiritual dimension (verse 10b). God expects *not mere* external obedience, but implants a new inward desire. He gives a new nature. The Holy Spirit indwells the believer and inclines him to obedience and to holiness in life and attitude.[106]

The promises of the old covenant were *earthly* and temporal. Obedience sprang from fear. The promises of the new covenant are *heavenly*, spiritual, and eternal. Obedience now is to issue from a willing heart and mind.

Under the new covenant there will not be any privileged class of priests who are given the task of teaching others. All distinctions of rank and importance under the new covenant will disappear (verse 11). God promised a new knowledge so that His people will know His laws, and He will give a new power so that His people can obey them.

God has been merciful to His people down through the years, but under the new covenant there will be a further

---

[106]   Irving Jensen, in a Sunday School discussion, said that one morning a young mother found an envelope on the breakfast table addressed to "Mommy." Ten new postage stamps were in the envelope, along with this note: "Dear Mommy, John is mad at you because you won't let us put our snowballs in the freezer, but I am not mad at you because I love you"—your friend, Colin.

extension of mercy (verse 12). The word "mercy"[107] may be translated "to have compassion," but it is really compassion in action. One of the most simple ways to think of mercy and grace (both of which are often used in the same setting), is to define *grace* as getting from God what we *do not* deserve, and *mercy* as not getting what we *do* deserve.

The new covenant is in effect now. Verse 6 says that Jesus "*is* [now the] Mediator of a better covenant." The same covenant will be experienced by Israel on a larger scale, and thus find its *complete* fulfillment at a future time.

The old covenant was based on the law God gave to Israel during the first part of their wilderness wanderings (at Sinai). The law was good, but it did not make man per-fect—so God inaugurated a new agreement.[108] For a while both covenants existed side by side, but the new covenant took over and the old began to disappear (verse 13).

God had made a covenant with the Children of Israel when He gave them the law at Sinai. He promised blessing to those who would "keep" His commandments. The old covenant was based upon something *that man should do*; the new covenant is based on something *that Christ has done*. Hebrews 8:6 says that Jesus is the Mediator of the better covenant. Its blessings belong to all who are trusting in Him

---

[107] *Mercy* is that aspect of God's love which causes Him to help the miserable, just as grace is the aspect of His love that moves Him to forgive the guilty. Those who are miserable may be so, either because of breaking God's law or because of circumstances beyond their control. God has shown mercy upon those who have broken His law (Daniel 9:9; 1 Timothy 1:13,16)...and mercy upon those who are miserable due to circumstances beyond their control...He healed blind men (Matthew 20:29-34) and lepers (Luke 17:11-19). See page 697, *Nelson's New Illustrated Bible Dictionary*.

[108] The Anabaptist theologian, J. C. Wenger, says that "the New Testament, especially the Book of Hebrews, indicates that the Old Covenant as a religious system has been done away; it has been superseded by its superior, the New Covenant" (*Introduction to Theology*, page 31).

and committed to living for Him.

The basic difference between the old covenant and the new covenant is that under the old, the sinner had to repeatedly present animal offerings to the Lord God (by way of the priest) to obtain the remission of sins. Under the new covenant, sinners are forgiven through the one-time sacrifice of Jesus on the cross.

The offerings of God's people under the new covenant are a combination of dedicated lives, and the desire to joyfully obey God's commands,[109] out of appreciation for the pardon He continually offers through Jesus' blood.

Gentiles have *not* fundamentally been a covenant people. Romans 9:4-5 indicates that the covenants are peculiar to Israel, but we know that Gentiles are recipients of the covenant blessings, for if we are members of Christ's family, we are *"Abraham's seed, and heirs according to the promise"* (Galatians 3:29).

All believers must acknowledge that *at times* they have broken God's laws, have lived selfishly, and have sometimes failed to seek God's will. At times we have lived as if there is no life beyond. In light of our failings, it is good to know that Jesus is our Advocate with God. He is the One who says, "Lord God, I have presented My life as a sacrifice for their sins. Because they have believed in Me, I ask that You grant them pardon."

Because of the work of Jesus in the believer's behalf, we

---

[109] The Anabaptists and Pietists held that the new birth must manifest itself in a new pattern of life. Philip Spener "considered all Scripture as God's inspired Word, but he held that the New Testament is a higher revelation than the Old Testament, because it fulfills the Old Testament. Thus the Christian experiences the New Testament more directly, and it raises man to a higher level" (*Background and Development of Brethren Doctrines*, Dale Stoffer, page 17).

can face the future with great confidence. F. B. Meyer wrote to a friend: *"I have just learned to my surprise that I have only a few days to live. It may be that before this letter reaches you, I will have entered the Palace. Don't trouble to write. We shall meet in the morning."*

2. The Furniture of the Tabernacle Described (9:1-5)

The author of Hebrews in this section lists the areas of the tabernacle and the pieces of furniture in it. In the early verses he does not go into detail, but gives this information to provide a setting for the thoughts which are forthcoming.

In the book of Exodus one finds the careful directions which God gave Moses for the building and setting up of the tabernacle. The full description of the tabernacle is found in Exodus, chapters 25-31, and the arrangement of the furniture in the tabernacle is described in Exodus 40. In the book of Leviticus exact directives are given for the ceremonies that were to be performed during the tabernacle services.

The writer names the various parts of the tabernacle and describes some of the pieces of furniture located in it.

a. The first part of the tabernacle (9:1-2)

(9:1-2) Then indeed, even the first covenant had ordinances of divine service and the earthly sanctuary. For a tabernacle was prepared: the first part, in which was the lampstand, the table, and the showbread, which is called the sanctuary;

The word "then" (verse 1) refers to the time when the first covenant was in force. The "ordinances of divine service" refer to the ritual which was connected with worship in the tabernacle. And even though *all this* was later done away, it did serve the purpose of instructing and blessing his people during the time for which it was appointed. The intent of verse 1 is not to ridicule the past, but to prepare readers to receive *the greater glories* contained in the new covenant.

God said to Moses, *"Make Me a sanctuary that I may dwell among them"* (Exodus 25:8). The tabernacle and all its furnishings were prepared (verse 2) according to the pattern that God showed him (Hebrews 8:5). The tabernacle itself was divided into two parts. The two-part tabernacle (or tent of worship) was surrounded by an outer court 150 feet long and 75 feet wide, which was enclosed by a curtain-like fence more than seven feet high. There was a single gate, 30 feet wide, on the east side of the outer court.

The first part of the tabernacle was usually called the *Holy Place,* the place where the priests performed their daily services. The *Holy Place* was a portion of the tent about 30 feet long, 15 feet wide, and 15 feet high. In the Holy Place ("the sanctuary") were furnishings including the lampstand, the table with the consecrated bread, and the altar of incense. The *lampstand* contained seven candles which illuminated the tent where the priests did their work. The *table* (Exodus 25:23-30) contained twelve loaves of bread (the *showbread*) which were placed there each Sabbath Day. Only the priests ate the bread, as specified in Leviticus 24:5-9.

b. The second part of the tabernacle (9:3-5)

(9:3-5) and behind the second veil, the part of the tabernacle which is called the Holiest of All, which had the golden censer and the ark of the covenant overlaid on all sides with gold, in which were the golden pot that had the manna, Aaron's rod that budded, and the tablets of the covenant; and above it were the cherubim of glory overshadowing the mercy seat. Of these things we cannot now speak in detail.

A curtain (or a "veil") separated the two parts of the tent of worship. Verse 3 speaks of "the second veil" because when the priests entered the tent from the outer court, there was a curtain (the first curtain), from the outer court to the

Holy Place. Then there was another curtain which separated the Most Holy Place from the Holy Place—and so, when the high priest entered the Most Holy Place (from the Holy Place) he went through the second curtain.

The second part of the tabernacle (verse 3), which was called the *Most Holy Place*, was the place where the living God promised to be. The *Most Holy Place* (known also as the "Holy of Holies," or the "Holiest of All"), was at the west end of the 45-foot-long tent—a portion shaped like a cube about 15 feet long, 15 feet wide, and 15 feet high. Only the high priest could enter this part of *the tent of worship*. Once a year, on the Day of Atonement, the high priest passed through the curtain into God's presence. The *Most Holy Place* contained the ark of the covenant (verse 4).

The *ark of the covenant* was a chest more than 3 feet long, 1 ½ feet wide, and 1 ½ feet high. It was overlaid on all sides with solid gold. The lid of the chest was known as "the mercy seat," and within the *ark of the covenant* were three items—the golden jar with manna, Aaron's wooden cane that gave fruit, and the tablets containing the Ten Commandments (Deuteronomy 10:1-5). The ark symbolized God's presence among His people, and the stone tablets were a reminder to Israel to keep the laws of God.

The altar of incense (verse 4a)[110] was sometimes called "the golden censer." It stood in the Holy Place outside the curtain which opened to the Most Holy Place, but *was carried inside the curtain* on the Day of Atonement. The smoke

---

[110] There is a seeming discrepancy in verse 4a. Hebrews 9:4 places the censer in the Most Holy Place, yet Exodus 40:26-27 places it in the Holy Place. The word "had" in the phrase "had the golden censer" is translated from a Greek word (*echousa*), which is the participial form of the Greek word *echo*. That word-form carries with it *the idea of use, not of place*. The censer was *used* inside the Most Holy Place, but was normally *kept* in the Holy Place in front of the curtain which leads to the Most Holy Place (Exodus 40:26-27).

of the incense concealed the mercy seat (the lid) on the ark so that the priest would not die (Leviticus 16:12-13).

Above the ark (verse 5) stood two angels carved out of gold (called cherubim), which faced each other, and had wings that spread out over the lid of the ark. They symbolized guarding the way to God. God promised to be enthroned between the two cherubim (1 Samuel 4:4; 2 Samuel 6:2; Psalm 80:1; Isaiah 37:16). But, the writer says, this is not the place to dwell at length on these furnishings, because there is *a reality* that has replaced the old tabernacle.

It is important to have a mental picture of the structure of the tabernacle and the worship practices connected with it, in order to understand the things mentioned in Hebrews 9.

"Let them make Me a sanctuary, that I may dwell among them" (Exodus 25:8)

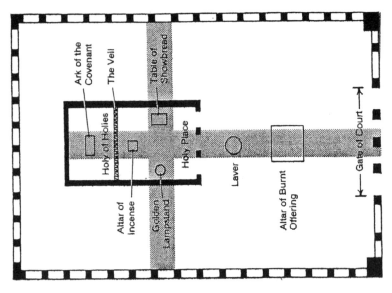

(Hebrews 9:11-12) "But Christ came as High Priest of the good things to come, with the greater and more perfect tabernacle not made with hands, that is, not of this creation. Not with the blood of goats and calves, but with His own blood He entered the Most Holy Place once for all, having obtained eternal redemption."

Believers know that the tabernacle, with its courtyard, was entered from the East. There was only one gate by which the priests could enter. The six pieces of furniture were arranged so that looking down from above reminded one of a cross—indicated by the shaded part on page 106.

Each piece of furniture had a typical significance. As noted, even the arrangement of the furniture in the tabernacle was positioned so as to form a cross, and was therefore a parable of the true sacrifice of Jesus yet to come.

The *altar of burnt offering* (in the outer court) was the place where the animals were sacrificed—a perfect picture of Christ, who Himself was a sacrifice for sin. The next piece of furniture in the outer court was the *laver (or basin)* where the priests could wash their hands after slaying the animal. The laver pictured Jesus who cleanses His people.

In the Holy Place there were three pieces of furniture. The *lampstand* pictured Jesus who lights the path of life; the *table with consecrated bread* pictured Jesus who sustains us day after day; and the *altar of incense* pictured Jesus' prayers interceding for us. He was the perfect Sacrifice becoming the perfect Intercessor for His people.

In the Most Holy Place there was one piece of furniture, the ark of the covenant. The lid of the ark (called "the mercy seat") was a symbol of God's forgiving nature. The ark of the covenant had three very special items in it.[111] The *golden pot containing manna* reminded people of God's miraculous provision for them during the wilderness journeys. Aaron's rod that budded was a sign of God's power. The two tablets of stone containing the Ten Commandments were reminders of God's laws for daily living.

---

[111] John Phillips likens *the pot of manna* to meeting physical needs, *the rod that budded* (dead wood that bore fruit) to meeting spiritual needs, and *the Ten Commandments tablets* to meeting moral needs (*Exploring Hebrews*, page 119).

3. The Services of the Priesthood Portrayed (9:6-10)

At this point the writer of Hebrews moves on from a description of the Old Testament tabernacle and its furniture, to an explanation of the duties of the priests, and then to the function of the high priest.

a. Restricted access to the presence of God (9:6-8)

(9:6-8) Now when these things had been thus prepared, the priests always went into the first part of the tabernacle, performing the services. But into the second part the high priest went alone once a year, not without blood, which he offered for himself and for the people's sins committed in ignorance; the Holy Spirit indicating this, that the way into the Holiest of All was not yet made manifest while the first tabernacle was still standing.

It was the duty of the priests (verse 6) to come into the Holy Place to carry out their daily ministry. The lamps were lighted (Exodus 27:20-21). The loaves of consecrated bread were replaced every Sabbath (Leviticus 24:5-9). The incense on the altar of incense was burned (Exodus 30:7-8).

Verse 7 explains that only the high priest, once a year, went into the Holy of Holies. Even in his high office, he could not go into the presence of God unaccompanied; he was to enter "not without blood"—which he offered for himself and for the unintentional sins of his people.[112]

The high priest, like all other humans, was a sinner, and so he could not enter the presence of God without blood. Before he entered into the Most Holy Place behind the veil, he divested himself of all his magnificent robes (Exodus 28:1-43), and put on a white linen robe (Leviticus 16:4), so

---

[112] Under the old covenant, the high priest could only make atonement for sins that were committed without intention to commit them ("the people's sins committed in ignorance"). No atonement was available for sins that were committed defiantly, intentionally, or presumptuously (Numbers 15:30-31). Numbers 15:22-29 speaks of the unintentional sins.

that he would stand before the Lord with nothing to offer but the blood of the slain animal.[113]

Verse 8 reminds readers that the Old Testament ceremonies had limited access to God's presence. For the common people, the way into God's presence was not yet truly made known. Ordinary people had no access to God, and even the ordinary priests were kept out of the inner sanctuary by a heavy curtain. Immediate access into the presence of God was not yet possible, and therefore fellowship with God was not yet perfect.

b. Partial cleansing by animal sacrifices (9:9-10)

(9:9-10) It was symbolic for the present time in which both gifts and sacrifices are offered which cannot make him who performed the service perfect in regard to the conscience—concerned only with foods and drinks, various washings, and fleshly ordinances imposed until the time of reformation.

Under the old covenant (verse 9), the conscience of many continued to be troubled because many sins could not be forgiven. No matter how many offerings or sacrifices a sinner might bring to God—his sin was not permanently gone. The ceremonial rituals did not cleanse the heart, and failed to bring a clear conscience to the worshiper—so there was no warm relationship with God spiritually.

---

[113] The high priest could never enter the Most Holy Place without the sacrificial blood of an animal. The high priest, on the Day of Atonement, went into the inner sanctuary twice—first with the blood of a bull, and then with the blood of a goat. He sprinkled the blood of the bull on the lid (the mercy seat) of the ark of the covenant, as a sin offering for himself and his household (Leviticus 16:11,14). After that he entered the Most Holy Place again with the blood of a goat which he sprinkled on the lid (the mercy seat) of the ark of the covenant for the sins of the people (Leviticus 16:15-16). After that, he laid his hands on another goat, confessed the sins of the people, and sent the goat far out into the desert, never to return. The Old Testament high priest prefigured Jesus, the divine and sinless High Priest whose blood made atonement for mankind.

The sacrifices of the old covenant were imperfect and temporary. But even though those sacrifices did not lead to a clear conscience nor produce spiritual life—they *did point forward* to Christ who could produce spiritual life.

The Old Testament "fleshly ordinances"[114] were "imposed until the time of reformation" (verse 10b). The meaning of the word "reformation" (Greek, *diorthosis*) is "to set things right." The word was sometimes used to describe the re-setting of broken bones.[115]

By way of summary—in Hebrews 9:1-10, the writer describes the operation of the Jewish tabernacle—the tent, the sacrifices, and the priesthood. Once a year the Jewish high priest would go into the Most Holy Place of the tabernacle (where the ark of the covenant stood) and there he offered the blood of bulls and goats for the sins of the people. God promised during the first covenant to meet human beings through the mediator—a human high priest.

The writer of Hebrews does not make light of the former system. He speaks of it with dignity, but he shows that the ritual and sacrifices of the old covenant were inadequate and temporary. The blood of bulls and goats could not (as Christ's blood did) accomplish eternal redemption for us. The old covenant itself was not inadequate, but the people failed to keep their part of the agreement.

---

[114] The "fleshly ordinances" speak of the Old Testament rules related to the human condition that included regulations about food, drink, and cleanliness. Those regulations did not cleanse the human heart; they were mere external and temporary arrangements.

[115] Kenneth Wuest says that the word *diorthosis* in its context here means "to bring matters to a satisfactory state. It refers to the introduction of the New Testament which later displaced the First Testament" (*Hebrews in the Greek New Testament*, page 156).

Chapter 8

OPERATION OF THE SECOND COVENANT
Hebrews 9:11—10:18

Many of the chapters in the book of Hebrews have one central message. Christ is superior to angels in chapter 1. Christ is superior to Aaron in chapter 5. Christ is a High Priest in the order of Melchizedek in chapter 7. And, in the last part of chapter 9, Christ offers Himself as a sacrifice for the human family and it is effective for all time.

Now, in the present age, Christ has come, and He is a High Priest of many good things that have come. By means of the heavenly sanctuary and by His own blood, He has obtained eternal redemption for mankind.

The sacrifice of Jesus on Calvary was not an annual event, but a single one-time event (9:11-12). Christ does not need to be crucified again. The Lord Jesus died "once for all" (9:12,26; 10:12,14). Christ's blood was shed for the remission of sins (9:26). Jesus stands now before the Father as an Advocate for His followers (9:24).

1. The Value of the Blood of Christ (9:11-28)

In this section of the letter, the old covenant and the new covenant are set side by side in order to show the defectiveness of the old covenant and the superiority of the new covenant which was inaugurated by the blood of Christ.

(9:11-15) But Christ came as High Priest of the good things to come, with the greater and more perfect tabernacle not made with hands, that is, not of this creation. Not with the blood of goats and calves, but with His own blood He entered the Most Holy Place once for all, having obtained eternal redemption. For if the blood of bulls and goats and the ashes of

a heifer, sprinkling the unclean, sanctifies for the purifying of the flesh, how much more shall the blood of Christ, who through the eternal Spirit offered Himself without spot to God, cleanse your conscience from dead works to serve the living God? And for this reason He is the Mediator of the new covenant, by means of death, for the redemption of the transgressions under the first covenant, that those who are called may receive the promise of the eternal inheritance.

Hebrews 9:11-15 speaks of "good things to come"[116] (verse 11); it speaks of a "more perfect tabernacle not made with hands;" it mentions coming "not with the blood of goats...but with His own blood" (verse 12); it says "the blood of Christ...[shall] cleanse your conscience" (verse 14); and, "He is the Mediator of the new covenant" (verse 15).

This passage centers on Jesus' death on the cross. The earlier chapters of Hebrews describe the Old Testament priesthood and the tabernacle and the sacrifices that were offered to seek the forgiveness of sin. This section of Hebrews *shows how Christ; by His sacrifice, has surpassed the institutions under the old covenant.* Many blessings have come to believers because of the sacrificial death of Christ.

Under the old covenant, the Jewish high priest entered into the Most Holy Place once a year with blood, to make atonement for himself and for the sins of the people. Yet he was inferior to Christ, whose priestly work on the cross has earned eternal salvation for those who believe the gospel message. The blood of Jesus was poured out as a single offering, and is eternally effective (verse 12b).

Verse 13 mentions "the ashes of a heifer" sprinkling

---

[116] There were trials and difficulties as believers traveled life's pathway, but there were *good things to come.* One of the good things that would come was the constant access into the presence of God because of the work of Jesus. Other good things, spelled out elsewhere in the Bible, include the redemption of our bodies, meeting with Christ, and eternal fellowship with God.

those who have been defiled. The ceremony is described in Numbers 19:2-9. A heifer was to be offered as a sacrifice, and its ashes were to be mixed with water, which then was sprinkled on those who were ceremonially impure. The purpose of the ritual was to symbolize "the purifying of the flesh" (verse 13b). Those who were sprinkled with the ashes mixed with water were fit again to engage in worship.

The blood of Jesus surpasses the animal offerings under the old covenant, for the writer says (verse 14), *"how much more shall the blood of Christ...cleanse your conscience* from dead works to serve the living God?" The blood of Christ is efficacious in that it produces the desired effect of making the conscience clean.[117]

Jesus' blood secures the forgiveness of sin. He became the Mediator of the new covenant (verse 15), and His blood

---

[117] Charles Colson, in his book *"Who Speaks for God?"* tells about Albert Speer, who was a technological genius working under Adolph Hitler, and was credited with keeping the German factories working during World War 2. After the war, he was the only one of 24 war criminals tried at the Nuremburg War Trials who admitted his guilt. Albert Speer spent twenty years in Spandau prison, and now he was writing a new book about his experiences during the war.

In one of his earlier writings Speer said, "The guilt can never be forgiven, or shouldn't be." An interviewer said to Speer, "So you *still* feel that way?" The look of sorrow and sadness on Speer's face was obvious as he responded. He said, "I served a sentence of twenty years, and I could say, 'I'm a free man; my conscience has been cleared by serving the whole time as punishment.' But I can't do that. I still carry the burden of what happened to millions of people during Hitler's lifetime, and I can't get rid of it. This new book is part of my atoning, of clearing my conscience." The interviewer pressed the point, and asked, "Do you really think you won't be able to clear your conscience totally?" Albert Speer shook his head and said, "I don't think it will be possible."

For many years, Albert Speer had accepted complete responsibility for his crime. His writings have been filled with contrition and warnings to others to avoid his mortal sin. He desperately sought expiation, but all to no avail. How sad—for indeed forgiveness and freedom of conscience is available through the blood of Jesus Christ. Coming to Christ and experiencing the new birth could have brought a new conscience, and Speer could have been cleared of lingering guilt. (Adapted from *Hebrews*, Kent Hughes, Volume 1, page 230).

is a ransom to free captives from their sin. His death was retroactive, and brought forgiveness for those who sinned, even in the days when the first testament (the old covenant) was still in effect (verse 15). With their blood offerings, they, in faith, *looked forward* to the coming Messiah; we, through faith, *look back* to the One who died for mankind.

One of the stanzas in the hymn, "Man of Sorrows," by Philip Bliss, expresses the truth about the blood shed by our great Mediator, the Lord Jesus Christ:

> *"Bearing shame and scoffing rude,*
> *In my place condemned He stood;*
> *Sealed my pardon with His blood;*
> *Hallelujah! What a Savior."*

There are those who speak disparagingly of the blood of Jesus, saying that those who speak about Christ's death and crucifixion, are promoting "a slaughterhouse religion." Yet when a catastrophe strikes and there are bloody injuries, they don't think of the blood banks that appeal for blood donations to save lives—as those who are speaking in terms of ugliness, horror, and the slaughterhouse.

(9:16-22) For where there is a testament, there must also of necessity be the death of the testator. For a testament is in force after men are dead, since it has no power at all while the testator lives. Therefore not even the first covenant was dedicated without blood. For when Moses had spoken every precept to all the people according to the law, he took the blood of calves and goats, with water, scarlet wool, and hyssop, and sprinkled the book itself and all the people, saying, "This is the blood of the covenant which God has commanded you." Then likewise he sprinkled with blood both the tabernacle and all the vessels of the ministry. And according to the law almost all things are purified with blood, and without shedding of blood there is no remission.

In verse 16 the writer states the fact that for a will to be in force, the testator[118] must die. A death was necessary for a will to take effect (verse 17). Verse 18 refers back to Exodus 24:6-8 where the act of Moses is described when he validated the old covenant by sprinkling sacrificial blood on the people and on the altar.

The *first covenant* was initiated and consecrated by blood, and the writer of Hebrews adds some details[119] that surrounded the inauguration of the first covenant (verses 19-21). The promise of cleansing and forgiveness came only when there was purging by shed blood. Verse 22 expresses the general conclusion that the law requires nearly everything to be cleansed with blood. The statement in verse 18b emphasizes the truth found in Leviticus 17:11, which says "it is the blood that makes atonement for the soul."

Scientists and doctors have enabled us to see blood as the body's source of life, and also as its cleansing and healing agent.[120] Blood provides the nutrients and the fuel to give strength to our body's cells. At the same time, the blood also carries away the waste materials and poisons.

Christ is the Mediator of the *new covenant* (verse 15a), and it was by His death that He was able to put the new and

---

[118] The word "testament" and "covenant" are the same in the Greek text. The word *testament* is used here in a legal sense, and the word *covenant* is used in a religious sense. A *testament* is a written document that provides for the disposition of one's personal property after death. A *covenant* is an agreement between two people (or groups) that involves promises on the part of each to the other. A testament (written by one or more persons) may be rewritten or changed, but the moment the maker of the will dies, the will is unalterable.

[119] Some details given here have not been spelled out in the Old Testament. These include descriptions about water, scarlet wool, hyssop, and the sprinkling of the vessels of the tabernacle with blood. Perhaps Exodus 24:6 is related.

[120] One doctor informed me (after I had several surgeries), that one of the reasons we are told to apply heat to a sore area of the body, is that *the heat draws an extra supply of blood* to the region—and the blood has healing qualities.

better covenant into operation. The Bible says, "The soul who sins shall die" (Ezekiel 18:4). Since the penalty for sin is death, nothing but death (symbolized by the shedding of blood) can atone for sin.

(9:23) Therefore it was necessary that the copies of the things in the heavens should be purified with these, but the heavenly things themselves with better sacrifices than these.

The tabernacle here on earth, and everything in it, is a copy of the heavenly sanctuary, and these things had to be made pure by the ritual sprinkling of blood (verse 23). The latter part of verse 23 does not mean that heaven itself needs cleansing, but that the heavenly sanctuary is made pure by a better sacrifice—the death of Jesus.[121]

(9:24-26) For Christ has not entered the holy places made with hands, which are copies of the true, but into heaven itself, now to appear in the presence of God for us; not that He should offer Himself often, as the high priest enters the Most Holy Place every year with blood of another—He then would have had to suffer often since the foundation of the world; but now, once at the end of the ages, He has appeared to put away sin by the sacrifice of Himself.

God's redemptive purpose for mankind is complete through the perfect sacrifice which Jesus made. He is not serving in an earthly tabernacle or temple, but has *now appeared* "in the presence of God for us" (verse 24).

We are reminded that the priesthood of Christ does not function in an earthly tabernacle, with sacrifices that are repeated over and over again, but that Christ was crucified

---

[121] Why does he say "better sacrifices" (plural), when obviously Jesus is *the* Sacrifice? The writer here (verse 23) is merely contrasting, in a general way, the *sacrifices* of goats and calves (under the old covenant), with the greatly superior *requirements* necessary for cleansing (under the new covenant), and the two plurals are a balanced grammatical fit for making the distinction.

once to make atonement for the sins of mankind, and that His work is in the sphere of the heavenlies (verses 24-25).

There are three great appearances of Christ mentioned in the final verses of Hebrews 9. Jesus "*has appeared* (past tense) to put away sin[122] by the sacrifice of Himself" (verse 26b). He entered heaven *"now to appear* (present tense) in the presence of God for us" (verse 24b). And to "those who eagerly wait for Him, He *will appear* (future tense) a second time, apart from sin, for salvation" (verse 28b).

The appearance of Christ in history to die for our sins speaks of His *incarnation*. The fact that Jesus is now appearing in heaven to be our Advocate with the Father, speaks of His *intercession*.[123] And the promise that He will appear a second time to complete our salvation, speaks of His future *revelation*.

(9:27-28) And as it is appointed for men to die once, but after this the judgment, so Christ was offered once to bear the sins of many. To those who eagerly wait for Him He will appear a second time, apart from sin, for salvation.

This passage contrasts the death of human beings and the death of Christ. The death of humans is appointed and judgment will follow. We cannot avoid death. It is a timeless truth—death once, and then the judgment.

---

[122] The magazine, *Consumer Reports*, published a small booklet entitled, "How To Clean Practically Anything." There is advice on which solvents one should use to remove many different kinds of stains. It is a useful little booklet, but it does not give any information about how to deal with the most serious stain of all—the ugly stains made by sin in our lives. The Bible has the answer. Jesus has "put away sin by the sacrifice of Himself" (Hebrews 9:26).

[123] The writer reminds readers that God's grace through Christ's intercession keeps flowing to us. Jesus knows our temptations, conflicts, and sorrows. He knows how we have faltered along the way. It is comforting to know that right now He asks that things might be prevented from happening to us (Luke 22:32). We are not to take a light attitude toward sin, but if in an unguarded moment, we do sin, we have an Advocate with the Father (1 John 2:1).

Unbelievers will be judged at the Great White Throne Judgment described in Revelation 20:11-12. The description of that judgment is one of the most solemn passages in the Bible.[124] Saved persons will be judged at what is sometimes called the Judgment Seat of Christ (2 Corinthians 5:10). All will stand before the Lord Jesus Christ to give an account of the things done in the body while on earth.[125] The knowledge of a coming day for the inspection of our lives should be a great incentive for right living.

For the Christian, there are several important observations about dying victoriously:

a. *While as believers, we prepare for death, death is not the central focus of our lives.* The central focus for us is the resurrection. We look to the day that Jesus will appear and abolish death, and transform our lowly bodies to be like His glorious body (Philippians 3:21). While we prepare for death, death is not the central focus of our lives.

b. *While we are burdened for those we love and leave behind at death, we recognize that our dying will be great gain.* When approaching the borders of death, we know that those who are left behind will be lonely. Hearing the news about a sudden death, or sitting by the bedside of one who is dying is always distressful. But when we arrive in the Paradise of God the mysteries of life will become clear.

---

[124] For more on *the judgment of unbelievers*, see the *BNTC Commentary on the Revelation*, pages 142-143. For additional information on the judgment of the unsaved dead and the Great White Throne Judgment, see the volume entitled, *Things to Come*, by J. Dwight Pentecost, pages 423-426.

[125] For more on *the judgment of the saved*, see the *BNTC Commentary on 2 Corinthians*, pages 64-65. Also, Wayne Grudem gives a detailed listing of the positive moral benefits of final judgment—including our inner sense of the need for justice, the provision of a powerful motive for righteous living, the incentive for believers to forgive others freely, and the furnishing of a great motive for evangelism. For an excellent summary of the many benefits of final judgment, see pages 1147-1153 in Grudem's *Systematic Theology*.

c. *While we enjoy life here on earth, it is enjoyed only temporarily, because we are ready to depart from it.* People of the world are not ready to depart from this life. If they do talk about the afterlife, it is mostly about Saint Peter with a bunch of keys. It seems that such comments are intended to hide some of the deep feelings of fear and uncertainty with which many unprepared worldlings are living.

The first part of verse 28 says, "So Christ was offered once to bear the sins of many"—a reference to the death of Jesus as a substitute for us. *His sinless life* qualified Him to be a suitable sacrifice for sin, but it was *His death* that made the payment for sin. He Himself "bore our sins in His own body on the tree, that we, having died to sins, might live for righteousness" (1 Peter 2:24).

Human beings are paupers before God. We are unable to meet the demands of a pure and holy God by our own cheap attempts to please Him. It is only when we see ourselves as poor lost sinful beings, and allow Jesus to remove the flimsy curtain of moral pretense, that we can be brought to a place where we acknowledge our need for help. It is only when we embrace the truth *that the blood of Jesus brings remission of sins*, that we receive the promise of an eternal inheritance (verse 15).

2. The Weakness of the Mosaic Law (10:1-10)

In this section the writer reaches his great climax. He brings to a conclusion the contrast between the Levitical priesthood of Old Testament times, and the great priesthood of Christ in New Testament times.

(10:1-10) For the law, having a shadow of the good things to come, and not the very image of the things, can never with these same sacrifices, which they offer continually year by year, make those who approach perfect. For then would they

not have ceased to be offered? For the worshipers, once puri-fied, would have had no more consciousness of sins. But in those sacrifices there is a reminder of sins every year. For it is not possible that the blood of bulls and goats could take away sins. Therefore, when He came into the world, He said: "Sacrifice and offering You did not desire, but a body You have prepared for Me. In burnt offerings and sacrifices for sin You had no pleasure. Then I said, 'Behold, I have come, in the volume of the book it is written of Me—to do Your will, O God.'" Previously saying, "Sacrifice and offering, burnt of-ferings, and offerings for sin You did not desire, nor had pleasure in them" (which are offered according to the law), then He said, "Behold, I have come to do Your will, O God." He takes away the first that He may establish the second. By that will we have been sanctified through the offering of the body of Jesus Christ once for all.**

The ceremonies under the first covenant *were impres-sive in many ways, but they never brought the worshipers into a permanent relationship with God.* If the ritual set forth in the Old Testament had made the worshipers perfect, those sacrifices could cease, because the worshipers would not any longer feel guilty for their sins (verses 1-2).

The animal sacrifices were not effective in removing sin, because they[126] were intended not so much to remove sin, as to foreshadow [127] the great sacrifice of Jesus. Only the one-time sacrifice of Christ could take away sin (Hebrews 9:26b), and abolish the consequences of sin permanently.

---

[126]   Early Brethren theologian, Peter Nead, had no doubts about the value of the blood of Christ. He quotes much of Hebrews 10:1-4 and then in commenting on the passage, writes, "Hence we learn that those sacrifices were not able to purge from sin. They could not produce a change in man; yet they were of great service to guilty man, for it was by the law of sacrifices that the great atonement which Christ, the Son of God, made in his own body…bearing our sins…by suffering a painful and shameful death" (*Nead's Theological Works*, page 21).
[127]   A "shadow" is a dim representation of the real thing.

In verses 5-10, the eloquent words of Psalm 40 are put into the mouth of Jesus at His incarnation. Jesus addresses the heavenly Father (quoting Psalm 40:6-8), and says that God no longer requires the repeated sacrifices of the old covenant. The blood of bulls and goats was not satisfactory, and so God made ready a body[128] for Jesus (verse 5b), who was obedient to the Father, ready to do His will (verse 7b), which was to give His life as a ransom for sin.

By those actions, the old system gave way to the new (second) covenant (verse 9), and God's will was effectively fulfilled in the sacrificed body of Christ. By the offering of His body, we have been sanctified—that is, made holy and acceptable to God (verse 10).

> *"Not all the blood of beasts*
> *On Jewish altars slain,*
> *Could give the guilty conscience peace*
> *Or wash away the stain.*
> *But Christ, the heavenly Lamb,*
> *Takes all our sins away,*
> *A sacrifice of nobler name*
> *And richer blood than they."*

God did not give the Hebrew people instructions about the sacrifices until He had first ordered them to obey His voice. In other words, *sacrifice* is no substitute for *obedience*. No offering is acceptable to God if it is not an evidence of loving devotion from the heart (verses 8-9).

God takes no delight in sacrifices. He is pleased instead

---

[128]   The author of Hebrews at this point quotes from Psalm 40:6-8, using the Septuagint translation, which speaks of a body prepared, instead of ears that have been opened. The special body which God prepared for the Messiah could indicate that Jesus may not have been genetically connected to either Joseph or Mary, and thus He was without sin. The birth of Jesus was normal, but His conception and the formation of His body were supernatural.

with the unfailing trust and obedience of His children. Jesus Himself demonstrated submission—a lesson for followers.

3. The Finality of Christ's Work (10:11-18)

This section of Hebrews 10 emphasizes the finality of Christ's sacrifice by contrasting it with the lack of finality of the Old Testament system of law and sacrifices.

(10:11-18) And every priest stands ministering daily and offering repeatedly the same sacrifices, which can never take away sins. But this Man, after He had offered one sacrifice for sins forever, sat down at the right hand of God, from that time waiting till His enemies are made His footstool. For by one offering He has perfected forever those who are being sanctified. But the Holy Spirit also witnesses to us; for after He had said before, "This is the covenant that I will make with them after those days, says the LORD: I will put My laws into their hearts, and in their minds I will write them," then He adds, "Their sins and their lawless deeds I will remember no more." Now where there is remission of these, there is no longer an offering for sin.

The first four verses of this section are a wonderful picture of Christ's perfect performance. Jesus of the new system is contrasted with the priests of the old system.

Three crosses were planted on the hill called Calvary. On the middle cross hung One who was not violent and profane, but the sinless Son of God. Barabbas went free that day, not because he was innocent, but because Jesus took his place. Jesus was crucified that day, not because He was guilty, but so that He could take the place[129] of Barabbas, and the place of every sinner who appeals for mercy.

In teaching the Lord's Prayer, Jesus gave an added admonition. He said, "For if you forgive men their trespasses,

---

[129] The blood atonement is clearly substitutionary (1 Peter 2:24).

your heavenly Father will also forgive you, but if you do not forgive men their trespasses, neither will your Father forgive your trespasses" (Matthew 6:14-15). Jesus, by His death, brings about the remission of sins, so that our sins and lawless deeds are no longer remembered (verse 17).[130]

The writer of Hebrews again demonstrates his high view of the Scriptures, by quoting two verses from Jeremiah and ascribes them to the Holy Spirit (verse 15). Verses 16-17 are quoted from Jeremiah 31:33-34.

The passage on the priesthood of Christ ends by enumerating many blessings—including an exalted priest (verses 12-13), an effective offering (verse 14), a new covenant in operation (verses 15-16), and a pardoned people (verses 17-18). William Cowper's hymn says it very well:

> *"There is a fountain filled with blood*
> *Drawn from Immanuel's veins;*
> *And sinners plunged beneath that flood,*
> *Lose all their guilty stains.*
> *The dying thief rejoiced to see*
> *That fountain in that day;*
> *And there may I though vile as he,*
> *Wash all my sins away."*

Under the old covenant, the Israelite could not even enter into the tabernacle (9:6-7), whereas the believer in Christ can now enter into the Holy of Holies (the very presence of God) with confidence, because God is pleased with the Calvary sacrifice of Jesus (10:19-20). Christ's perfect sacrifice annuls the old order, and therefore no need exists for a further offering for sin (10:18).

The writer of Hebrews has now reached the end of his argument about the superiority of Christ's person and work.

---

[130] God forgives and forgets our sins and "lawless deeds," and in the same way we are to forgive those who sin against us (Ephesians 4:32).

If, in Christ, we have forgiveness and the promise of eternal life through faith in His blood sacrifice, there is no need at all to continue the former system of sacrifices.

Christians today must be careful not to become morally careless. The function of the law and the sacrifices in Old Testament times was to remind Israel of the sinfulness of sin, and how badly they needed forgiveness. The Day of Atonement was an annual reminder to Israel of every person's need of cleansing.

Under the new covenant, the suffering and death of Jesus should be a reminder of the fact that each of us is a helpless sinner, and in need of forgiveness. But the excruciating suffering of Jesus on the cross not only reminds believers of the seriousness of sin—it also produces the removal of guilt for having sinned. To be justified is to be declared just as if we had not sinned.[131]

It is important for believers to think often of Calvary, and the tremendous cost of their salvation. Each time we participate in the lovefeast experience, and especially the bread-and-cup communion service, we are reminded of the price Jesus paid in order that we might be forgiven.

The work of sacrifice is done. There will be no more provisions made for the redemption of mankind. Forgiveness is already available for those who trust in the great sacrifice which Jesus made. Christ's death makes the Old Testament sacrifices obsolete. The one single offering of Christ has wiped out the need for the sacrifices in the old system, and has introduced a new era.

---

[131] See the *BNTC Commentary on Romans*, chapter 5, which is entitled "The Justification of Sinners." Note especially the explanation of the meaning of justification on pages 63-64.

Part III
THE SUPERIOR PRINCIPLES OF CONDUCT
Hebrews 10:19—13:25

Chapter 9
USE THE NEW ACCESS TO GOD
Hebrews 10:19-39

The third major section of Hebrews begins with an appeal to readers, urging them not to give up the benefits of Christ's work as High Priest. Believers are to "draw near" to God with a true heart. We are not to hold on to any secret bitterness, or envy and jealousy of any kind. When God looks at our lives He looks for devoted hearts.

1. Let Us Draw Near (10:19-22)

Christians are encouraged to "draw near" (come to God intimately and frequently) with a sincere heart, in full assurance of faith, freed from an evil conscience.

(10:19-22) Therefore, brethren, having boldness to enter the Holiest by the blood of Jesus, by a new and living way which He consecrated for us, through the veil, that is, His flesh, and having a High Priest over the house of God, let us draw near with a true heart in full assurance of faith, having our hearts sprinkled from an evil conscience and our bodies washed with pure water.

The words, "to enter the Holiest by the blood of Jesus, by a new[132] and living way" (verse 19)—mean that Jesus opened a path for us to come into God's presence.

Under the old covenant, the "veil" was the curtain that separated the Holy Place from the Most Holy Place of the tabernacle. Under the new covenant, the "veil" is a type of man's sinfulness—but Christ's broken body ("His flesh"), sacrificed on the cross, opened the way into God's presence.

---

[132] We have confidence to enter the Holy of Holies (the presence of God). Under the old system people were forbidden to enter the sanctuary of the tabernacle, but Christians may now enter God's presence by the shed blood of Jesus.

In light of the new open access, believers are encouraged to draw near to God—to come to Him intimately, and to do it frequently with a sincere heart.[133] We are to come to Him in confidence and with freedom from a guilty conscience (verse 22)—and we can do that because of the "new and living way" provided through the blood of Jesus.

The reference to "our bodies washed with pure water" (verse 22b) is not a *clear* reference to baptism (although it could be interpreted that way). It more likely has reference to purification rites found in the Old Testament, which were only hazy symbols of the purity and righteousness which believers possess because of the blood of Jesus.

Under the old covenant, the curtain closed the way into the Most Holy Place (the place where God promised to be). Only the high priest could enter, and only on one day of the year. Under the new covenant, the way has been made open for any of the Lord's disciples at any time. The hindrance is removed, and we have full access into the Holiest.

2. Let Us Hold Fast In Hope (10:23)

When the writer of Hebrews urges believers to "hold fast the confession of our hope," we are reminded to be open and public with our testimony of faith in Christ.

(10:23) Let us hold fast the confession of our hope without wavering, for He who promised is faithful.

The present tense of the verb "hold fast" our confession suggests the importance of *continuing to give voice* to our faith, and to do it without becoming apologetic or hesitant. The words of the Psalmist are related to this plea: "Let the redeemed of the Lord say so" (Psalm 107:2).

---

[133] Verse 22 speaks of approaching God, and "the emphasis falls on the triad of a [cleansed] heart, [a pure] body, and [an undefiled] conscience" (Robert Ross in *The Wycliffe Bible Commentary*, Pfeiffer and Harrison, page 1420).

The word translated "hope" (verse 23) is *elpis*, which according to Thayer[134] was the word for "trust" that is used in the Greek (*Septuagint*) translation of the Old Testament. The word refers to a joyful and confident expectation of everlasting salvation in the eternal world.

The phrase "without wavering" means that we are not to vacillate back and forth between various positions, but to know what we believe and to stand for those convictions at all times. Believers can maintain such a sure hope because the God who promises salvation always has been, and always will be, faithful to keep His promises.

One of the great needs in our communities today, is for God's people to witness to their faith, and to live it out, facing life's frustrations in a Christ-like manner.

3. Let Us Not Forsake the Assemblies (10:24-25)

Apparently some, even in the early days of the church, were neglecting[135] to fellowship with the other saints in the regular times of worship and Bible study. Verses 24-25 are a clear command to assemble with other Christians.

(10:24-25) And let us consider one another in order to stir up love and good works, not forsaking the assembling of ourselves together, as is the manner of some, but exhorting one another, and so much the more as you see the Day [of the Lord] approaching.

The word "consider" means to think of one another, and to encourage one another. The phrase "to stir up" (verse 24) means "to stimulate" or "provoke"—in this case, to love and

---

[134] *Thayer's Greek Lexicon*, page 205.

[135] The phrase "not forsaking" (Greek, *enkataleipontes*) the assembling together is a reference to the neglect, and the abandoning, of the practice of meeting with other believers. The same word is used of Jesus' cry of desertion on the cross, as recorded in Matthew 27:46. Jesus cried out, "My God, My God, why have You forsaken (deserted or abandoned) Me?"

to good works. When we see the zeal of fellow Christians, and share in their trials, and rejoice in their joys—it gives us new courage to press on in the Christian journey of life.

It is essential that God's people attend the scheduled services of the local body, in order to experience communion with the saints, to partake of the ordinances, and to receive thoughtful exhortations from the Word.

Sunday morning radio messages may be a blessing, but listening to the radio at home is not a substitute for assembling with others when meetings are called.[136]

It is not unusual—when inviting unsaved people to come to a church service—to get a response indicating that there are too many hypocrites in the church. But hypocrites buy groceries too, and that doesn't keep those folks from buying groceries at the same store. Hypocrites use banks, but those who excuse going to church services because of hypocrites, have accounts in the same banks. Hypocrites work in factories and shops, but that does not keep most people from going to work day after day.

The church on earth has always been imperfect. It was imperfect before our cradles were made, and it will be imperfect after our coffins are rotted. Our purpose for gathering together is to help promote in each other's lives—the virtues and graces that we covet for ourselves.

God shares His gifts with His children, and not all have the same gifts. We will most likely meet other children of God in the assembly of His people, to whom He has shown some truths which He has not shown to us—and we can benefit from hearing others. We have a high calling to en-

---

[136] The difference between listening to a radio sermon, and going to a church service, is about the same as the difference between talking to one's girl-friend on the phone, or spending the evening with her! Most young men know that actual presence with their special friend will always surpass a mere phone call.

gage in encouraging one another, and to stimulate one another spiritually and morally.[137]

For every believer, there will be crises that eventually come—and in the dark and difficult days, each member of the local body can benefit from the encouragement and support of other faithful men and women of God.

George Guthrie tells about the giant redwood trees in northern California. They have a relatively shallow root system. Their enormous weight is supported in part by the interlocking of a tree's roots with the roots of other trees around it. Guthrie concludes by saying, "As Christians we need 'interlocking roots' with other believers in the church to withstand the enormous weight of life. We need others spurring us 'on toward love and good deeds' in a world so bent on self-centeredness and self-gratification."[138]

Every sincere Christian should be able to sing Timothy Dwight's hymn with gusto:

> *"I love Thy kingdom, Lord,*
> *The house of Thine abode;*
> *The church our blest Redeemer saved*
> *With His own precious blood."*

Assembling together for public worship was a regular feature of the early church. In those early decades of the New Testament era, Christians "continued steadfastly in the apostles' doctrine and fellowship, in the breaking of bread, and in prayers" (Acts 2:42).

The concluding clause in verse 25 ("so much the more

---

[137] Leslie Flynn tells about the elderly man who could be seen walking to church every Sunday morning. Neighbors knew he was almost deaf, and couldn't hear a word of the sermons. A scoffer wrote out a question one day and showed it to him when he was on his way to church. The question was this: "Why do you go to church each week when you can't hear a word?" He quickly responding by saying, "I want my neighbors to know which side I'm on."

[138] *The NIV Application Commentary: Hebrews*, page 352.

as you see the Day approaching"), is a reminder that the day of our Lord's return continues to draw closer. The writer is speaking of the Second Coming of Christ—the day when the saints will rise to meet the Lord in the air. The appeal is that we keep our hearts bathed in repentance and cleansed from sin—holding fast to our profession of faith.

4. *Fourth Warning Passage—Danger of Willful Sin (10:26-31)*

This is a warning passage which urgently admonishes and warns against the willful sin of rejection. There is an awful fate awaiting those who persist in sin and in rejecting Christ after they have once received the truth.

(10:26-31) For if we sin willfully after we have received the knowledge of the truth, there no longer remains a sacrifice for sins, but a certain fearful expectation of judgment, and fiery indignation which will devour the adversaries. Anyone who has rejected Moses' law dies without mercy on the testimony of two or three witnesses. Of how much worse punishment, do you suppose, will he be thought worthy who has trampled the Son of God underfoot, counted the blood of the covenant by which he was sanctified a common thing, and insulted the Spirit of grace? For we know Him who said, "Vengeance is Mine, I will repay," says the Lord. And again, "The LORD will judge His people." It is a fearful thing to fall into the hands of the living God.

These verses contain a warning that resembles the words of Hebrews 6:4-6. Neglecting the assembling with God's people can lead eventually to a rejection of Christ's sacrifice for sin.

For a background to these verses, it will be helpful to read several Old Testament passages. A *background to verse 26* can be found in Numbers 15:30, which says, "The person who does anything presumptuously...brings reproach on the Lord, and he shall be cut off from among his people." A *background to verse 28* can be found in Deuteronomy 17:6, where we read, "Whoever is deserving of death shall be put to death on the testimony of two or three witnesses; he shall not be put to death on the testimony of one witness." And *a background to verse 30* can be found in Deuteronomy 32:35-36, which says, "Vengeance is Mine," and again, "For the Lord will judge His people."

The fourth warning passage (10:26-31) is about the sin of apostasy—a deliberate rejection of the truth of the gospel of Jesus Christ. [139] Those who apostatize—defiantly renounce Christ and the power of His cleansing blood. They mock and jeer at His ability to save. The argument in verses 28-29 is this: If rejecting the way of truth in Old Testament times brought dire punishment (verse 28),[140] what kind of punishment might one suppose will be given for those who trample under foot the blood atonement of the Son of God (verse 29)? The transgressor will die unforgiven!

Because Jesus, by His death on the cross, has provided *the only* acceptable sacrifice for sin—*there is no other sacrifice—no other way to come to God.* Some of the Hebrews had become Christians, but were considering reverting back to Judaism and its temple-sacrifices under the old covenant. Those *who willfully sin* by defiantly rejecting Christ's blood atonement as the way of salvation—will discover that there no longer "remains a sacrifice for sins."

Those early Christians, who planned to leave Christ and return to Judaism, apparently to avoid persecution, were heading for God's terrifying judgment. The writer of Hebrews says that anyone who rejects the sacrifice of Christ

---

[139] We need to remember that a temporary backsliding is very different from apostasy, which is a deliberate and determined action of the mind to renounce the blood of Christ as the way of salvation.

[140] What could be worse than dying "without mercy" (verse 28)?

for the forgiveness of sin will find no other means of receiving pardon. *Those who reject the blood atonement of Christ to find salvation—are spurning the only way God has provided to remove sin!*

There remains no more sacrifice for sins. God has no additional means of atonement held in reserve. *Buddhism's* elimination of desire, *Hinduism's* series of reincarnations, and *Islam's* loyalty to the laws of Allah, will not provide for the removal of sin.

It is a very serious matter to trample under foot the Son of God, and to treat as "a common thing"[141] the blood of the covenant by which he was set apart (verse 29). It insults the Holy Spirit when we make light of what He has said about Jesus, and when the atoning blood of Jesus is rejected.

In the earlier chapters of Hebrews, the writer has very convincingly shown the superiority of Christ's sacrifice to atone for the sins of humanity. Now, the writer says, to show scorn for that act—is to willfully invite judgment from "the hands of the living God" (verse 31).

5. Another Reminder to Persevere (10:32-39)

Christians had been suffering bitter persecution; now they must be careful not to throw away their earlier confident faith. Some form of the word "endure" is used in verses 32, 34, and 36. Just as believers trusted Christ to save them, so they need to trust Him to meet each day's problems—and maintain a mindset to endure.

(10:32-34) But recall the former days in which, after you were illuminated, you endured a great struggle with sufferings: partly while you were made a spectacle both by re-

---

[141] The KJV says "an unholy thing," but the word literally means that which is common or ordinary, treating Christ's blood as no better than any other blood. Preachers who diminish the value of Jesus' blood are guilty of sacrilege.

proaches and tribulations, and partly while you became companions of those who were so treated; for you had compassion on me in my chains, and joyfully accepted the plundering of your goods, knowing that you have a better and an enduring possession for yourselves in heaven.

The writer now changes the tone of his words, going from a stern warning to a pleading appeal. The readers are urged to remember the days after their conversion, when they firmly stood for their convictions, even though sometimes they were exposed to insult and persecution.

Many students of church history believe that the passage refers to the time when the Jews were expelled from Rome under Claudius in 49 A.D.

While those who received the letter to the Hebrews were not themselves in prison, they did sometimes visit others who were in prison because of their faith. Visiting fellow believers who were in prison openly identified those who did the visiting as Christians, and they themselves became subject to arrest and ridicule (verse 33).

Some of the readers had experienced the loss of their property. Their material goods were plundered and confiscated, yet their fervor for the Lord was so great that they "joyfully accepted the plundering" of their goods (verse 34), knowing that they had "a better and an enduring possession...in heaven" (verse 34b).[142]

(10:35-39) Therefore do not cast away your confidence, which has great reward. For you have need of endurance, so that after you have done the will of God, you may receive the promise: "For yet a little while, And He who is coming will come and will not tarry. Now the just shall live by faith; But

---

[142]   Richard Taylor says, "When our sole treasure is in the 'here and now,' and our faith in the future is feeble, we cannot rejoice when persecution uproots us" (*Beacon Bible Commentary*, Volume 10, page 134).

if anyone draws back, My soul has no pleasure in him." But we are not of those who draw back to perdition, but of those who believe to the saving of the soul.

It was the confidence which the early Christians had in the faithfulness of God that enabled them to endure much suffering (verses 35-36). It is important to persevere in the faith, for believers are assured in James 1:2-4 that God develops the trait of patience (perseverance), through trying circumstances in the lives of those who trust Him.

The Christians were aware that, at any moment, the Lord may come (verse 37)—and when He comes, He will rescue and deliver His people.[143] We should be able to endure ridicule and even loss of property—because we know that God will come through with His protection, and ultimately with a reward in Heaven.

We come to God by faith; we enter into the kingdom by faith; we receive forgiveness by faith; we are to live day after day by faith (verse 38). But those who "draw back" from believing in the efficacy of Christ's atonement are destined for perdition. The word "perdition" means utter destruction. It is a description of Hell.

God gives human beings the awesome ability to make choices. We can commit ourselves to Christ, or we can draw back. We can accept the living God as being true, or we can be persuaded that He is false. Our decision will determine whether we *live* or *die* for all eternity. There is an awful fate awaiting those who persist in the sin of rejecting Jesus Christ after they have received the truth. Hopefully, readers of this commentary are "not of those who draw back to perdition" (verse 39).

---

[143]   The quote in verse 37 is a combination of truths from the *Septuagint* (Greek translation) of Isaiah 26:20 along with part of Habakkuk 2:3.

Chapter 10

REMEMBER FAITHFUL FOREBEARS-1
Hebrews 11:1-19

We have arrived now at one of the most familiar chapters of the Bible. Some earlier parts of the book of Hebrews are difficult to understand—but the accounts of the courageous people described here are inspiring, and they encourage us to continue on with the journey.

Faith is the quality which accepts what it cannot understand. William Barclay says, "Into life, for everyone, at some time, there comes something for which there seems to be no reason...something which defies explanation. It is then that a man is faced with life's hardest battle—that battle to accept what he cannot understand. At such a time there is only one thing to do—to submit, to accept, to obey; and to do so without resentment and without rebellion, saying, 'God, Thou art love! I build my faith on that.'"[144]

Hebrews 11 is a marvelous sermon about those who endured—strengthened by their faith in the true and living God. Biblical *faith* means trusting God. It is a simple act of the will. The faith of the Bible heroes described in Hebrews 11 should bring encouragement to all believers who have declared their loyalty to Jesus Christ.

Hebrews 11 is known as the great "faith chapter" of the Bible. The word *faith*, as used in the Bible,[145] is not a blind leap in the dark, but it is accepting as very real, all those things which have been spoken and presented in the Word

---

[144]   William Barclay, *The Letter to the Hebrews*, page 173.
[145]   Christians believe the Bible is trustworthy for many reasons. The reasons include the testimony of archaeology, the Bible's fulfilled prophecy, the transforming power of the Scriptures, and the testimony of Jesus.

of God. Dedicated Christians are convinced that the Bible is a book they are to live by and die by, and that its statements are true and trustworthy in all parts.

1. The Description of Faith (11:1-3)

The word "faith" has a number of facets of meaning. It is one of the ingredients by which we come into the Christian life and receive the forgiveness of sins[146] (Ephesians 2:8). Galatians 3:26 says that we are "sons of God *through faith* in Christ Jesus." The Apostle Paul said that he was "crucified with Christ," nevertheless he lived "*by faith* in the Son of God" (Galatians 2:20).

(11:1-2) Now faith is the substance of things hoped for, the evidence of things not seen. For by it the elders obtained a good testimony.

The New Testament word that is usually translated "faith" is *pistis*, meaning *a firm belief or conviction based on truth as given in the Word of God.* Faith accepts as true, what God has said, and then acts on it. In the spiritual life, *faith* must be *as natural and ongoing*, as is our breathing in the physical life.

Objects in the physical world can be seen with the human eye, but convictions about things which are invisible are produced by faith (verse 1). *Faith is a firm conviction*

---

[146] In Brethren circles, Dale Stoffer says, "By the 1840s discussions had arisen over *the proper order* of repentance and faith [with regard to accepting Christ and becoming a Christian]. Some Brethren maintained that a degree of faith *must precede* repentance in order for a change of heart to take place, while others insisted that there could be no true, saving faith without repentance" (*Background and Development of Brethren Doctrines, 1650-1987*, page 109). In 1844, the Brethren Annual Meeting was asked to resolve the issue. Its answer included a quote from Hebrews 11:6, and then said: "Out of this faith, when it is quickened, repentance will come" (*Minutes of the Annual Meetings of the Brethren from 1778-1909*, page 83). In other words, the position held by the early Brethren was that generally speaking, faith precedes repentance.

about the reality of things which we cannot see. It does not take faith to see a tree if one is walking through a forest. But to believe the unexplainable, and to accept as real those things which we cannot see, requires faith. By faith we believe the unseen, because someone in whom we have confidence says that it is so. Real biblical faith rests upon the authority of God's Word.

The term "elders" (verse 2) refers to the great heroes of Old Testament times. These were men and women of faith who had a good testimony, because, when faith was put to a test in their lives, they reached out and grasped the unseen world, and found that it is very real. The faith manifested by the catalogue of early saints led to worthy deeds, and verse 39 repeats the thought found in verse 2.

(11:3) By faith we understand that the worlds were framed by the word of God, so that the things which are seen were not made of things which are visible.

The writer of Hebrews begins his description of faith by making a comment about creation. No one was present at the time of creation to observe God as He created the world. It is only as we believe the account in the inspired Scriptures, that we can obtain a true understanding of the wondrous works of creation. The visible creation (things we can see) testifies to its invisible Creator (whom we cannot see). Faith points each individual to an unseen power Who made the world as we see it all about us.

Christians must take a stand on the Word of God when discussing the origin of the universe. Our knowledge about the forming of the universe is based *on faith* (verse 3)—that is, on a faith which believes that the Word of God is authoritative and true in all its parts. As Christians, we are sure that the creation of the worlds occurred by the word of the living God, but we were not there to see it.

Young persons in almost any secular university today will be ridiculed, if not actually persecuted, if they hold the creationist view of the origin of the universe. Yet, to discuss origins is simply outside the scope of science.[147] The college science professor who presumes to speak about the origin of the universe—is no longer speaking as a scientist, but as a philosopher. Evolution is not a science; it is a religion. The evolutionary view of the world's origin, and the biblical Christian faith, cannot be harmonized.

2. Three Clear Examples of Faith (11:4-7)

The three early examples of faith were ordinary men, who by God's grace were able to do extraordinary things. Each man was a sinner who made some mistakes and at times grieved the Lord—but each exemplified faith in the true God in spite of the unbelief all around them.

a. Abel, the worship of faith (11:4)

(11:4) By faith Abel offered to God a more excellent sacrifice than Cain, through which he obtained witness that he was righteous, God testifying of his gifts; and through it he being dead still speaks.

Abel must have had instruction from God regarding the kind of offering he should bring.

Abel's sacrifice of a lamb from his flock represents the true approach to God in worship, in contrast to Cain's offering the product of his fields. The "way of Cain" (Jude 11) stands for a bloodless, humanistic religion. God was pleased

---

[147] The British zoologist, T. H. Huxley, popularized Darwin's evolutionary theories. But toward the end of Huxley's life, he was honest and confessed an important truth. He said: *"It appears to me that the scientific investigator is wholly incompetent to say anything at all about the first origin of the material universe"* (quoted from T. H. Huxley, in an article in *Nineteenth Century*, February, 1886, page 202, by John Philips in *Exploring Hebrews*, page 161).

with Abel's offering; it foreshadowed the offering of the Lamb of God which takes away sin (John 1:29).[148]

Abel offered a sacrifice which was more acceptable to God than that which was presented by his brother Cain. Abel offered not only the best gift (a blood-offering from the firstlings of the flock), but also, he gave a sincere offering. Even though Abel was murdered by his brother Cain, Abel's life still has spoken over the centuries.[149]

Abel worshiped God in God's way, by faith when he lived, and that faith makes him speak now that he is dead.

b. Enoch, the walk of faith (11:5-6)

(11:5-6) By faith Enoch was taken away so that he did not see death, "and was not found, because God had taken him"; for before he was taken he had this testimony, that he pleased God. But without faith it is impossible to please Him, for he who comes to God must believe that He is, and that He is a rewarder of those who diligently seek Him.

Enoch leaped from this life right into the next, and was one who bypassed the grave. To live for 300 years in constant fellowship with God, as Enoch did, was a great triumph for faith (Genesis 5:22).

Genesis 5:24 reports, "Enoch walked with God, and he was not, for God took him." Enoch lived in an age of much corruption, but his life was pleasing to God. Enoch stood out as a man of righteousness; and as a result "God took

---

[148] John Phillips explains the contrast: "Cain's religion was one of good works and human merit. According to him…he must pay the price. He offered to God the fruit of the earth, the product of his labors, the sweat of his brow, his toil and self-effort. His religion…ignored…the shedding of blood. Abel, on the other hand, brought a lamb [and] took his stand as a hopeless sinner needing a Saviour and a Substitute; and slew his lamb, shedding its blood to show his willingness to approach God in God's way" (*Exploring Hebrews*, page 162).

[149] Early Brethren writer, L. W. Teeter, says: "Abel's worthy sacrifice shows his excellent faith…he was even mentioned by the blessed Son of God in Matthew 23:35" (*New Testament Commentary*, Volume 2, page 396.)

him" so that he did not experience death. The Bible records only one other such event—that of Elijah (2 Kings 2:11).

Verse 5 says that Enoch, when God had taken him, "was not found." Often it is not until saints are gone, that others realize what a spiritual giant the person was. Enoch was missed so much that friends tried to find him. (When Elijah was taken alive into heaven, fifty men [2 Kings 2:16-18] searched for him.)

Enoch did not always walk with God. Genesis 5:21-22 says that Enoch lived 65 years before Methuselah was born, and *"after he begot Methuselah, Enoch walked with God"* for the remaining 300 years of his life. It could be that the birth of that little boy, along with the responsibilities of parenthood, caused Enoch to take eternal values seriously.

The Genesis account says that Enoch "walked with God," and the writer of Hebrews says that his walk pleased God (verse 5). That thought led the writer to one more observation about pleasing God. It is impossible[150] to please God "without faith." Righteous living cannot exist without faith. A person of faith will believe that God exists (verse 6), and that He rewards those who *diligently* seek Him, that is, they seek Him with an earnest purpose.

c. Noah, the work of faith (11:7)

(11:7) By faith Noah, being divinely warned of things not yet seen, moved with godly fear, prepared an ark for the saving of his household, by which he condemned the world and became heir of the righteousness which is according to faith.

Noah's ark was a work of faith. He built the vessel on dry land, and had likely never seen a ship floating on water,

---

[150] The text does not say that without faith it is *difficult* to please God, but that without faith it is *impossible* to please Him. No believer, upon his deathbed, has ever said, "I would have been happier if I had served the world."

rising and falling on the waves. But he believed God, and in godly fear[151] he set out to do exactly what he was told to do.

God specifically warned Noah that a flood was coming and Noah took the warning seriously, built an ark according to the instructions he received, and his family was saved from the gushing waters. Noah offered an ongoing obedience to God, and through his obedience his household was saved, while all others perished.

Noah was "a preacher of righteousness" (2 Peter 2:5). The people in Noah's community must have ridiculed him time and time again for building a huge ark made to float, long before any rains came. In spite of the ridicule, Noah was a good example of a believer who trusted God, was eager to hear what God was saying, and was ready to do what God was commanding.

Noah lived in times when "the wickedness of man was great in the earth" (Genesis 6:5), but "Noah found grace [favor] in the eyes of the Lord" (Genesis 6:8). Only Noah and his family were saved from destruction. That may seem like a rather poor showing for more than one hundred years of preaching—but Noah's straight preaching "condemned the world"—and our generation, like Noah's generation, does not relish the message of judgment. Preachers today are often guilty of softening the message of judgment.

All three of the illustrations in verses 4-7 describe the triumph of faith over death. Abel's faith illustrates that the death of a substitute is the gateway to eternal life. Enoch's faith points to a triumph over death, for he did not experience death. Noah's faith saved others from death.

---

[151] The word "fear" is *eulabeomai*, which means "to act cautiously, to reverence, and to stand in awe of." Noah did not act under the influence of fright. Adapted from *Hebrews in the Greek New Testament*, Kenneth Wuest, page 199.

3. The Faith of Abraham and Sarah (11:8-19)

Abraham had already appeared in Hebrews 6:13-15 as an example of one who through faith and patient endurance "obtained the promise."

a. The promised land (11:8-10)

Though Abraham did not know where he was going, God knew, and that was enough for this man of faith.

(11:8-10) By faith Abraham obeyed when he was called to go out to the place which he would receive as an inheritance. And he went out, not knowing where he was going. By faith he dwelt in the land of promise as in a foreign country, dwelling in tents with Isaac and Jacob, the heirs with him of the same promise; for he waited for the city which has foundations, whose builder and maker is God.

There are three distinct times when Abraham's faith was clearly evident. First, God asked him to go to a land that He would show him, a place that God would give to him as an inheritance (verse 8). In faith, Abraham left his father's household, not knowing where the Lord would lead.[152]

Abraham's stay in Canaan was temporary. He was a stranger living in tents (verse 9). Abraham, and his son and grandson ("heirs with him of the same promise") spent a long time living in tents, not in cities or houses.

By faith, Abraham knew that his earthly dwelling could not be compared with the heavenly city which God Himself was building (verse 10). He knew, by faith, that long after the cities in the land of Canaan had crumbled into dust, the city God was preparing would stand.[153]

---

[152] As we grow older, sometimes we must move from a familiar past to an uncertain future—sometimes to a smaller place, to a daughter's home, or even to a nursing home. We may not know the road, but we know Who is with us.

[153] Cities on earth are often destroyed. We think of Pompeii (in Italy), Knossos (in Crete), Sodom and Gomorrah, Dunwich (English port city that slid into the sea), and the massive destruction of New Orleans (in the year 2005).

b. The promised son (11:11-12)

God had promised that He would make a great nation from Abraham's offspring. When Abraham was one hundred years old, *Isaac* was born—and fifteen years before Abraham died, his grandsons *Jacob and Esau* were born. And although Abraham did not live long enough to see his descendants become as numerous as the stars in the sky, it is true that God's promise was kept.

(11:11-12) By faith Sarah herself also received strength to conceive seed, and she bore a child when she was past the age, because she judged Him faithful who had promised. Therefore from one man, and him as good as dead, were born as many as the stars of the sky in multitude—innumerable as the sand which is by the seashore.

Sarah's faith was not like Abraham's, but it was a true faith, and God was well pleased. Through faith, Sarah was changed from a barren woman to a joyful mother. She came to believe what at first she had laughed at as impossible. Actually, since husband and wife are one—by faith, Abraham, together with Sarah, received the power to become parents of a child. The Apostle Paul links both Abraham and Sarah together in Romans 4:19.

The result of Abraham's faith was that from one man many descendants were born—a great multitude, as numerous as the stars in the sky, and as countless as the sand on the seashore (verse 12).[154] This promise has symbolically been true of Abraham's natural descendants, and it is also true in a spiritual sense, for Abraham is "the father of all those who believe" (Romans 4:11).

---

[154] Dr. Henry Morris says that astronomers have statistically estimated that there are about 10 million billion billion stars in the known universe—that is 10 to the 25th power in mathematical language. See *The Biblical Basis of Modern Science*, pages 156-158.

c. The test of faith (11:13-19)

God called Abraham to sacrifice his son Isaac because God wanted to test Abraham's faith.

(11:13-16) These all died in faith, not having received the promises, but having seen them afar off were assured of them, embraced them and confessed that they were strangers and pilgrims on the earth. For those who say such things declare plainly that they seek a homeland. And truly if they had called to mind that country from which they had come out, they would have had opportunity to return. But now they desire a better, that is, a heavenly country. Therefore God is not ashamed to be called their God, for He has prepared a city for them.

These verses contain a parenthetical thought. All the people named so far believed that the promises to them would be fulfilled, although only at some future time.

All of the men listed were still living by faith when they died. They had not given up, but persevered until the end. Even though they were pilgrims and strangers on earth, they "all died in faith" (verse 13a). As a result, they longed for "a heavenly country" (verse 16). The Christians in Jamaica have a favorite chorus; with fervor, they sing, *"Oh my, what joy and bliss, heaven's goina be better than this."*

Christians desire something better than this world. It has never satisfied us. This world seemed to bring a temporary satisfaction when we were dead in sin, but no person will find the perfection of heaven here on earth.

The Old Testament saints would have had opportunities to return to their earlier homelands (verse 15), but they were not even glancing back! They were too excited about the future which lay ahead!

(11:17-19) By faith Abraham, when he was tested, offered up Isaac, and he who had received the promises offered

up his only begotten son, of whom it was said, "In Isaac your seed shall be called," concluding that God was able to raise him up, even from the dead, from which he also received him in a figurative sense.

Abraham's trust in God's integrity was so great that he felt perfectly safe to obey absolutely, and to leave to God the ways and means by which things would work out.

Abraham did not actually sacrifice Isaac (verse 17), yet God said he did "offer up Isaac"—because *God knew that he really would have slain Isaac,* had the animal not been available to offer as a substitute.[155] This was a very severe test because all the promises of God to Abraham were wrapped up in Isaac (verse 18; Genesis 21:12b). How could God keep His promise to give Abraham descendants through Isaac if he obeyed the command to slay him? But, by faith, Abraham obeyed.

Abraham was willing to offer his son Isaac as a sacrifice to God, in confidence that God would bring him back to life. Abraham believed that God was able to resurrect ("to raise up") dead bodies (verse 19). Abraham may have reasoned that if God could give life to an infant (and cause Isaac to be born) from the seed of an aged man, He could likewise perform a second miracle, and bring his son Isaac back to life after his death.

The faith chapter (Hebrews 11) presents us with a simple message that must not be tossed to the side: *The life of faith is the only life that pleases God.*

---

[155] Sometimes young children in a Christian family press to give their hearts to Jesus very early in life. Parents are uneasy about encouraging them to receive baptism and having them officially become members of the church when they are perhaps only five or six years old. God knows the sincerity of the child's heart and will bring the sincere child to the point of church membership in due time. This passage assures us that God knows the decision and will honor it until that time when a more mature step is taken to be received into the local body.

In the first part of Hebrews 11, the reader is given a *description* of faith. Earlier in the book of Hebrews, the author had introduced *the concept of faith* when he spoke of the disobedient Israelites. He said they heard the message of the gospel, but it *was not combined with faith* in the hearts of those who heard it (Hebrews 4:2).

The writer of Hebrews then gave some *examples* of persons who lived by faith in the early history of mankind, including the faith of Abel and of Enoch and of Noah. Abel sacrificed by faith. Enoch walked by faith. Noah worked in faith. Had it not been for faith, Noah would likely have agreed with his neighbors, that boat-building was a strange hobby, in a land where water was not abundant.

The next twelve verses in Hebrews 11 make observations about Abraham's faith. Abraham's faith triumphed in three areas. The *first* was Abraham's obedience in moving to a new and unknown country. The *second* was his faith in believing that God would enable Sarah to bear a son even in her old age. The *third* was the command that Abraham was to sacrifice his son Isaac, for God wanted to test his faith.

God expects His people to be persons of faith. If all that we are, and have, and do—differs little from our unbelieving neighbors—then we have embraced their values, and we are deceiving ourselves by declaring that we are living for another world and under the leadership of another King. Our lives are to be ordered by the values of a heavenly kingdom, bearing witness to standards found in the Bible.

Faith accepts without having all the facts.

Unbelief rejects in spite of the facts!

Chapter 11

REMEMBER FAITHFUL FOREBEARS-2
Hebrews 11:20-40

The *first section* of Hebrews 11 informs readers about the faith of Abel, Enoch, Noah, Abraham, and Sarah. In *this section*, we learn about the faith of Isaac, Jacob, Joseph, Moses, Moses' parents, Joshua, Rahab, and other unnamed heroes who trusted in the living God.

1. The Faith of Isaac, Jacob, and Joseph (11:20-22)

The writer of Hebrews moved rapidly through the next three generations that followed Abraham. It would be difficult to find three men who are more different from each other, than these three. But all were men of faith who blessed others, and who themselves were blessed.

In these verses the author of Hebrews unfolds an interesting description of the patriarchal blessings.[156] In the case of Abraham's sons—*not Ishmael*, but Isaac received the blessing. In the next generation, *not Esau*, the firstborn, but Jacob, received the covenant blessing. In the next generation, *not Reuben*, the firstborn, but Joseph received the blessing by way of his sons, Manasseh and Ephraim.

a. Isaac blessed Jacob and Esau (11:20)

(11:20) By faith Isaac blessed Jacob and Esau concerning things to come.

Isaac was the son of a famous father (Abraham), and he

---

[156] The "blessing" was *not simply* the father conveying his "best wishes" to the son, but was the means by which the son was to be linked with the blessings promised to Abraham, including the land of Israel, and the family through which someday the Messiah would come. When the blessing was once given, even if spoken by mistake, it could not be taken back (Genesis 27:33).

was the father of a famous son (Jacob, later called "Israel"), yet Isaac himself lived a rather ordinary life.

In his earlier years, Isaac knew that God had ordained that the patriarchal blessing was to go to Jacob, the younger son (Genesis 25:23b), but Isaac tried to give the blessing to Esau, who was his favorite of the two sons. Since Esau was the firstborn, he should have received both the birthright[157] and the blessing, but he sold his birthright (Genesis 25:29-34), and as a result, lost the blessing.

In Hebrews 11:20, however, God commends Isaac's faith for blessing *both* Jacob and Esau when he spoke of their future, as recorded in Genesis 27:27-40. Note especially verses 38-40. Isaac was so old and blind that he could not tell one of his sons from the other, but he was willing, by faith, to accept God's intent to give the greater blessing to the younger son, Jacob, contrary to the standard practice of giving the greater blessing to the firstborn son.

b. Jacob blessed the sons of Joseph (11:21)

(11:21) By faith Jacob, when he was dying, blessed each of the sons of Joseph, and worshiped, leaning on the top of his staff.

Unlike Isaac, Jacob was a master schemer. At birth, he grabbed his twin brother by the heel, and throughout his life, he attempted to trip up anyone who tried to interrupt his plans. He was not at all like his father, Isaac.

The incident in the life of Jacob which is mentioned here occurred when he was old, blind, and infirm. The text omits any reference to the blessings that Jacob pronounced

---

[157] The "birthright" was a privilege to which the firstborn son was entitled by birth in Bible times. The firstborn son enjoyed a favored position. His birthright included a double portion of his father's assets upon the father's death (Deuteronomy 21:17), a special blessing from the father, and traditionally the privilege of leadership in the family (*Nelson's Illustrated Bible Dictionary*, page 184).

on *his sons*, as he predicted the future (Genesis 49:1-27). Instead, the writer selects the incident when Jacob gave a blessing to *his grandsons*.

When Joseph, with his two sons, came to Jacob, Joseph was given the blessing of the firstborn. This was not a double portion of Jacob's herds and flocks, but a double portion of the promised land of Canaan.[158] When pronouncing the blessing, Jacob crossed his arms, and contrary to the normal practice, gave Joseph's younger son, Ephraim, the blessing of the firstborn. Ephraim later became a leader in Israel, and was so dominant that the ten tribes in the northern kingdom were often called *Ephraim*.

The mention of Jacob's "staff" is interesting. It had been Jacob's companion through the years. With the staff, he had crossed the Jordan (Genesis 32:10). He had leaned on his staff when he came back from the place of his wrestling with the angel (with God), limping because of his dislocated hip (Genesis 32:22-32). It was fitting that he should lean on the same staff as he worshiped in old age.

c. Joseph foretold his death and burial (11:22)

(11:22) By faith Joseph, when he was dying, made mention of the departure of the children of Israel, and gave instructions concerning his bones.

Only good things can be said about Joseph. He was *persecuted* by his brothers, but refused to carry a grudge against them. He was *tempted* to commit fornication with Potiphar's wife, but he fled lest he sin against God. Is Joseph the son of scheming Jacob? Yes, but at times one wonders where Joseph got his integrity?

The fact that Joseph, near the time of his death, wanted

---

[158] Actually, Joseph himself did not receive the blessing, but each of his two sons (Ephraim and Manasseh) received the blessing. They became two tribes of Israel because Jacob accepted the two sons of Joseph as his own sons.

his bodily[159] remains carried back to the land of Israel was sure proof that he believed that God's people would later be delivered out of Egypt. So, all through the long years of wilderness wandering, Joseph's bones were carried along as a reminder that the God who brought them out of Egypt would bring them safely into Canaan.

Joseph never forgot that he belonged to God's chosen nation. He refused to become an Egyptian. He was seventeen years old when he was taken to Egypt, and was thirty years old when he became the second ruler in the land—so he had spent thirteen years under pagan Egyptian influence. Yet he remained a man of faith in the true God. Joseph was an Israelite and he wanted to be buried with his brethren in the land of their inheritance.

2. The Noteworthy Faith of Moses (11:23-29)

This section deals with the place of faith in the life of Moses. Several phases of his life are mentioned in these verses, including his birth, his identification with the chosen people after having been reared and educated by the daughter of Pharaoh, and his involvement with the first Passover and the crossing of the Red Sea.

a. Moses' parents (11:23)

(11:23) By faith Moses, when he was born, was hidden three months by his parents, because they saw he was a beautiful child; and they were not afraid of the king's command.

---

[159] God is concerned about the human body. One day God's people will have new bodies—a body like Christ's glorious body. In our day, many are resorting to cremation as a way of disposing of dead bodies. Cremation of the body seems like a cruel and barbarous act, yet the Bible does not directly condemn cremation. For a more careful study of cremation, see *BRF Witness*, Volume 41, Number 1, January-February, 2006, pages 11-12. Write to Brethren Revival Fellowship, Box 543, Ephrata, PA 17522 and request a free copy.

The Scripture (Exodus 2) describes the hiding of baby Moses by his parents. The text here mentions two aspects of their action. First, they saw that Moses was no ordinary child, and second, they were not afraid of the king's edict which required the death of Hebrew baby boys by casting every male infant into the Nile River (Exodus 1:22).

Amram and Jochebed sensed that this child was *proper* (KJV), that is, "beautiful,"[160] in the sense of being exceptional, and seeming to have a special destiny. There is a hint here that the parents had a degree of prophetic insight—and this gave them courage to believe that if God had a special plan for him, He would protect the child.[161]

When the child became so active and noisy that they could no longer keep his presence secret, they prepared a floating cradle and assigned his older sister Miriam to be his "baby sitter." Without being terrified by the commandment to destroy all the male babies, they acted boldly and defied[162] the king's command.

b. Moses, the leader (11:24-29)

(11:24-26) By faith Moses, when he became of age, refused to be called the son of Pharaoh's daughter, choosing rather to suffer affliction with the people of God than to enjoy the passing pleasures of sin, esteeming the reproach of Christ

---

[160] The descriptive word "beautiful" (NKJV) is the translation of the Greek word *asteion*. Acts 7:20 translates the same word by saying that Moses was "well pleasing to God." The parents likely had some prior word from God, or they could not have acted "by faith." In their estimation, and in the plan of God, Moses was comely and was destined to be used for an outstanding service.

[161] And indeed Moses was the man God chose to write the first five books of the Bible, to lead Israelites out of the bondage in Egypt, etc.

[162] This does not imply that the people of God may defy any civil law that they happen to dislike (such as a seat-belt law), but even before the Ten Commandments were given, Moses' parents knew it was wrong to kill, to slay their child. The Bible truth is that when the law of man is contrary to the clear Word of God, Christians must choose to obey God rather than man (Acts 5:29).

greater riches than the treasures in Egypt; for he looked to the reward.

These verses commend Moses' faith. By faith, Moses was able to perceive what the most important issues in life were. On the surface it appeared as if he were choosing between pain and pleasure; but in reality, Moses was choosing between godliness and sinful living.[163] Likely his mother Jochebed had cautioned Moses many times when he was a young child about the sinfulness of much that was commonly approved in Egyptian society.

Moses could have had all the glittering pleasures of Egypt, but he chose instead "to suffer affliction with the people of God" (verse 25).[164] The pleasures of sin quickly pass, lasting only "for a season" (KJV)—and then they are all over. The "reward" (verse 26) includes the benefit of a good conscience here in this life, and the permanent blessing of a home in the eternal world.

Robert Burns described passing pleasures:
"But pleasures are like poppies spread;
You seize the flower, its bloom is shed;
Or like the snow that falls on the river,
A moment white, then it melts forever!"

---

[163] The fact that Moses chose to remain faithful to the God of Israel, says something about the influence of his godly mother during the early years of his training. Moses' decision to identify with the people of God was his personal choice, but Moses learned the issues at stake while a little child at his mother's knee. The influence of Jochebed was so great that all the training in the king's court could never erase it. A mother has untold influence on her children. The proverb contains much truth: "The hand that rocks the cradle rules the world."

[164] The British preacher, Charles Spurgeon, describes the condition of the people of God in Egypt as "wretchedly poor, engaged in brick-making, and utterly spiritless. They were literally a herd of slaves, broken down, crushed, and depressed. Only faith could have led Moses to side with them. Moses teaches us to take our place with those who follow Christ and the Scriptures" (*Spurgeon's Commentary on Great Chapters of the Bible*, page 312).

Some will likely ask, "How could Moses identify with 'the reproach of Christ' (verse 26), when Christ[165] had not yet come?" The word "reproach" speaks of *ridicule, slander, and all kinds of blasphemous treatment* at the hands of unbelieving people.

We remember how Peter winced when the servant girl said to him, "You also were with Jesus of Galilee" (Matthew 26:69). Peter's denial on that occasion was later reversed when he stood before the Jewish Sanhedrin and declared, "We cannot but speak the things which we have seen and heard" (Acts 4:20). Serving Christ often brings ridicule and treatment which is much more severe.[166]

By faith, Moses could see the truth expressed in the New Testament: *"For I consider that the sufferings of this present time are not worthy to be compared with the glory which shall be revealed in us"* (Romans 8:18).

Most certainly there were many pressures designed to

---

[165] Nineteenth century Brethren writer, L. W. Teeter, explains: "It appears that Moses was born to be the deliverer and leader of Israel. As such he became a type of Christ, of which he himself speaks (Deuteronomy 18:15); however, not by name, but plainly by character, which Peter confirms (Acts 3:22-26)...Hence Moses—as Christ's type...may properly be regarded as having suffered reproaches with Christ, whilst delivering and leading Israel to Canaan" (*New Testament Commentary*, Volume 2, page 400).

[166] The primitive church knew something about "the reproach of Christ," as did the Waldenses, the Reformers, the Wesleyans—and most of all, the Anabaptists. More Anabaptist Christians died during the sixteenth century than did the early Christians in the first century. J. Denny Weaver describes just one incident. He says, "At the turn of the year to 1527, Michael Sattler...[was] to take charge of the Anabaptist congregation at Horb on the Neckar River. Within a few days of his arrival there, Sattler, his wife, and a number of other individuals were arrested by Austrian authorities and imprisoned in Rottenberg. The trial occurred on May 17-18, 1527. The execution on May 20, 1527 displayed particular cruelty. Sattler's tongue was cut out and his flesh torn numerous times with hot tongs. He was then burned at the stake. Two days later Margaretha...was drowned in the Neckar River in Rottenberg" *(Becoming Anabaptist: The Origin and Significance of Sixteenth Century Anabaptism*, pages 61-62).

keep Moses from leaving the palace of the Pharaohs. If Moses had stayed in Egypt, he may have become a noted statesman, and perhaps could have made some changes for the enslaved Hebrews. The argument would be this: by remaining in the government he could present the cause of his people. But Moses was not inclined to become an Egyptian diplomat; his aim was to be a loyal man of God.

(11:27-29) By faith he forsook Egypt, not fearing the wrath of the king; for he endured as seeing Him who is invisible. By faith he kept the Passover and the sprinkling of blood, lest he who destroyed the firstborn should touch them. By faith they passed through the Red Sea as by dry land, whereas the Egyptians, attempting to do so, were drowned.

The word "forsook" (Greek, *katelipen*) means "to leave behind once and for all" (verse 27). The king of Egypt was angry at Israel's departure, so he determined to call up his army and bring the Israelites back to Egypt. Moses did not fear "the wrath of the king" because he believed in the promises made by the invisible[167] God. Indeed, God stepped in and parted the waters of the Red Sea.

It certainly required faith on the part of Moses and his people to obey the instructions of the Passover. How could the blood of a lamb sprinkled on a doorpost, protect a household from death? Why should they apply blood to the door using a flimsy little bush called hyssop? Moses and his people believed God's promise and "kept[168] the Passover and the sprinkling of blood" (verse 28).

The focus here has been on *the nation* Israel. The Israelites shared Moses' vision. They applied the blood to the

---

[167] God is spirit and thus is not a material being. He is invisible to the physical eye, *but not* to the eye of faith. He is no less real because He is invisible.

[168] Kenneth Wuest says that "the word 'kept' is the translation of *poieo* [a word that means] 'to make.' which in this context means 'to institute'" (*Hebrews in the Greek New Testament*, page 208).

doorposts and kept the Passover. It was not only Moses who believed in God's word. The nation Israel, along with Moses (recorded in Exodus 14:13-22), also displayed noble faith as "they" safely "passed through the Red Sea as by dry land" (verse 29). The Egyptians, who were following close behind, were drowned (Exodus 14:23-28).

3. The Faith of Joshua and Rahab (11:30-31)

The writer of Hebrews passes over the years of wandering in the wilderness,[169] and takes us to the story with the first primary difficulty the Hebrews had when they reached the borders of Canaan. Even though the Israelites had crossed the Jordan River, the city of Jericho was a massive fortress which barred the way into the Promised Land.

(11:30-31) By faith the walls of Jericho fell down after they were encircled for seven days. By faith the harlot Rahab did not perish with those who did not believe, when she had received the spies with peace.

Jericho was located at the eastern border of Canaan, and nomadic tribes from the desert to the East would sometimes try to invade the land. The heavily-walled city of Jericho often prevented invaders from entering the main valleys of Canaan. The people inside the walls had plenty of water and vast storehouses of food, so they could survive onslaughts that lasted for a lengthy period of time.

When the Israelis arrived at the border of Canaan, God told Joshua, "I have given Jericho into your hand, its king, and the mighty men of valor" (Joshua 6:2). God gave instructions telling Joshua what to do, and by faith, Jericho fell.

---

[169] Warren Wiersbe says, "Between verses 29 and 30 are forty years of Israel's wandering in the wilderness; yet not one word is said about it. Why? Because those were years of unbelief, and Hebrews 11 celebrates faith" (*Run With the Winners: A Study of the Champions of Hebrews 11*, page 113).

Day after day the people marched around the walls of the well-fortified city—until, on the seventh day, they marched around the walls seven times. Then the trumpets were blown, the people shouted, the walls fell, and the city was taken.

In the city of Jericho, there lived a prostitute named Rahab. The writer of Hebrews had identified a long list of godly men, beginning with Abel, then Enoch, Noah, Abraham, Isaac, Jacob, and Moses. Then in the midst of the list of heroes of faith, he inserts the name of Rahab the harlot.

Rahab was a pagan woman. She was not familiar with the law of God. She did not have the benefit of being a part of the nation Israel and its special relationship with the true God. She heard about the victories He gave to the Israeli people—and even though it was primitive, Rahab had faith that Israel's God is the God of heaven and earth. She came out from her pagan culture and allied herself with God's people when she hid the spies (Joshua 2:1-22).[170]

By the grace of God, Rahab became an ancestress of the Lord Jesus Christ (Matthew 1:5). God accepted this woman who had been involved in sinful living and a pagan way of life—because of her willingness to trust His word. The Apostle James commends her faith (James 2:25).

4. Other Heroes of Faith (11:32-40)

The list of heroes of faith is coming to a close. There simply is not enough time to keep on naming additional heroes. In this section the writer tells about the heroic deeds of some who were faithful (verses 32-33), and also about some of the cruel sufferings of those who stood firmly for the Lord (verses 34-38).

---

[170] Rahab's faith was clearly expressed in her confession, as it is recorded in Joshua 2:9—"I know that the Lord has given you the land."

a. Some who triumphed (11:32-33)

(11:32-33) And what more shall I say? For the time would fail me to tell of Gideon and Barak and Samson and Jephthah, also of David and Samuel and the prophets: who through faith subdued kingdoms, worked righteousness, obtained promises, stopped the mouths of lions,

In verse 32, the writer mentions names from several periods of Israel's history. The list includes some from the period of the judges (Gideon, Barak, Samson, and Jephthah); the period of the kings (David); and from the time of the prophets (Samuel and "the prophets").

In this list of names, there are some who were characterized by serious faults and obvious flaws. The one thing that set them apart was their simple faith. Though God did not excuse their faults, He did honor their faith.

Gideon was a spiritual leader who with 300 men delivered Israel from the oppression of the Midianites. Gideon was noted for his visions and the way he was given signs.

Barak refused battle against Sisera unless Deborah went with him (Judges 4:8). Barak fought the Canaanites and defeated them (Judges 4:16).

Samson had a love affair with Delilah which has placed a blot on his name, yet he manifested faith in Israel's God when he prayed for strength to mete out justice on the enemies (Judges 16:30).

Jephthah made a rash vow that compelled him to sacrifice his own daughter (Judges 11:39-40), yet God used him to defeat the Ammonites. He was a man of faith.

David was a capable musician, noted statesman, respected king, and a spiritual leader. Because he trusted God, he was able to conquer enemies and strengthen the nation.

Samuel was the last of the judges and first of the prophets. He was a generous and faithful man. He traveled from place to place and taught the Word of God faithfully.

In verse 33, the writer no longer lists the *names* of the heroes of faith, but summarizes a variety of *deeds* that were accomplished by faith.

There were those who *subdued kingdoms*. Certainly Joshua did when he led the Israelites in conquering the Promised Land. David conquered the nations surrounding Israel and extended its borders.

The phrase *worked righteousness* carries with it the concept of performing acts of righteousness. When Elijah challenged the prophets of Baal, and defeated them—that was an act of righteousness. It was an act of righteousness when Elisha gave the formula for healing Naaman.

Some *obtained promises*, likely referring to Abraham who was promised a son, and to the men and women of Israel who were promised a new land (Exodus12:25), and a redeemer who would be the Messiah (Isaiah 53:1-12).

Others *stopped the mouths of lions*, including Samson, who tore a lion to pieces with his hands (Judges 14:6), and David, who rescued a sheep from the mouth of a lion (1 Samuel 17:34-37), and Daniel, who was protected from the lions in the den when God sent an angel to shut their mouths (Daniel 6:21-22).

b. Some who suffered (11:34-38)

(11:34-38) quenched the violence of fire, escaped the edge of the sword, out of weakness were made strong, became valiant in battle, turned to flight the armies of the aliens. Women received their dead raised to life again. And others were tortured, not accepting deliverance, that they might obtain a better resurrection. Still others had trial of mockings and scourgings, yes, and of chains and imprisonment. They were stoned, they were sawn in two, were tempted, were slain with the sword. They wandered about in sheepskins and

160

goatskins, being destitute, afflicted, tormented—of whom the world was not worthy. They wandered in deserts and mountains, in dens and caves of the earth.

Those who *quenched the violence of fire* refer to the three friends of Daniel who accepted the burning, fiery furnace instead of bowing in worship to the image of the pagan king of Persia (Daniel 3:1-25).

Those who *escaped the edge of the sword* include David who was threatened on several occasions by the envious King Saul. Hezekiah, king of Judah, knew that the Assyrian army was marching toward Jerusalem, but because of his faith in God, learned that an angel slew 185,000 enemy soldiers in just one night (2 Kings 19:35).

There were some who *became valiant in battle* and turned armies to flight, including Gideon and Samson and Barak and Jephthah. It is interesting to note that Jephthah was the ninth judge of Israel. He was an illegitimate child and was cast out of his family by his half-brothers, yet God used him to win a mighty victory against the Ammonites (Judges 11:32-33).

There were women who received *their dead raised to life again* (verse 35). The reference is to Elijah raising the widow's son (1 Kings 17:17-24), and to Elisha raising the son of the Shunammite woman (2 Kings 4:8-37).

At this point, the writer of Hebrews goes from naming *specific examples* of faith, to more *general occurrences* of torture and trial because of faithfulness to God.

Some *were tortured, not accepting deliverance* in order that "they might obtain a better resurrection" (verse 35b). These were persons who suffered in various ways and did not experience miraculous escapes. Down through the years there were some men and women of faith who were treated worse than animals. That does not mean that God failed them. Those unnamed heroes of faith glorified God just as much as those who were miraculously delivered. One group glorified God *by escaping danger*; the other group glorified God *by remaining faithful* in the midst of trial.[171]

Still others *were mocked and scourged and chained in prisons* (verse 36). Many times they could have recanted and regained their freedom, but they kept their eyes on those things which are eternal.

Some *were stoned* (verse 37). We think immediately of Stephen, one of the first deacons in the church age, and the first Christian martyr. Stephen was stoned to death (Acts 7:57-60), and as he was dying, he asked God not to charge his persecutors "with this sin" (Acts 7:60).

Others *were sawn in two*, undoubtedly referring to the tradition that Isaiah met death by this means. Some *were tempted*, as for example, was the case with Joseph when propositioned by Potiphar's wife. Some *were destitute and afflicted and tormented*, wandering about in sheepskins and goatskins (verse 37b). They were ill-treated, sometimes surviving in deserts and mountains and caves (verse 38).

c. Many are commended (11:39-40)

(11:39-40) And all these, having obtained a good testimony through faith, did not receive the promise, God having provided something better for us, that they should not be made perfect apart from us.

The faithful ones described in Hebrews 11 were men and women who believed God and looked forward by faith to a coming day when all of God's promises would be fulfilled in the eternal world.

The Old Testament saints manifested faith *in a promise*;

---

[171] George Guthrie says, "It is striking that in the list of Hebrews 11, we do not have one healing, although support for that form of miracle can be found elsewhere in the New Testament" (*The NIV Application Commentary*, page 389).

the New Testament saints had faith *in a Person*. The saints from former times were promised a home in Heaven, on credit, so to speak.

The Old Testament saints gained approval as a result of their faith, but they did not receive the realization of Christ's complete salvation, or the fulfillment of the New Covenant with its blessings. They died before Christ came, but they believed something better still lies in the future. This perfection will come for both Old and New Testament saints when Christ returns to complete salvation and to reign as King of kings and Lord of lords.

In the Bible, the saints from Old Testament times, along with the saved from New Testament times, are considered one family, and a family is not really complete unless *all* the family members are there. God has "provided something better [than this life] for us, that they should not be made perfect apart from us" (verse 40). What a day that will be, when in the realms of heaven, we meet with the stalwart heroes of faith who have inspired us in this life.

It is important that followers of Christ do not come to believe that the Christian life is a kind of insurance policy guaranteeing that we shall be free from the troubles of life. God is all powerful, and certainly *can* deliver us from every harsh thing that might come our way—but sometimes in His wisdom He will see fit to allow us to face hardships.

Christians today are to take "the shield of faith" and use it "to quench all the fiery darts of the wicked one" (Ephesians 6:16). The "shield" used in New Testament times was a large piece of wood or metal that was placed in front of a soldier and moved in such a way that it would protect the whole body. Foot soldiers would often wrap the pointed tips of arrows with pieces of cloth, soak them in pitch, set them on fire, and then shoot them toward the enemy.

Spiritually, the "fiery darts" speak of fierce temptations, deep doubts about God's goodness, strong sweeping sexual passions, and dark discouragement. Such "fiery darts" are often sent our way. Like the heroes of faith, we too need to exercise faith to be among the winners on the spiritual battleground. Faith is the power to keep on believing the truth of God's Word, no matter what comes our way. Faith can quench the darts of temptation. Faith in the true God believes there is a crown at the end of the road.

An observation was made in the previous chapter:

God expects His people to be persons of faith. If all that I am and have and do—differs little from my unbelieving neighbors—then I have embraced their values, and I am deceiving myself by saying that I am living for another world, and under the leadership of another King. My life is to be ordered by the values of a heavenly kingdom, which bears witness to the standards found in the Bible.

As we look at the list of heroes named in Hebrews 11, we are inspired by their heroic deeds, but we realize too that each was a faulty human being. We remember that one time Noah was drunk and lay naked in his tent; Abraham lied about Sarah, and Isaac lied about Rebekah; Moses committed murder, and the Children of Israel were repeated grumblers. Gideon was a doubter and David was an adulterer. Yet in this chapter each of these persons was considered a hero because each manifested faith in the true and living God. They looked forward to sharing the realms of heaven—not because they were perfect, but because they believed in the great promise that "God will raise up for you a Prophet" (Deuteronomy 18:15), whom Peter understood to be a reference to the Messiah, the Lord Jesus (Acts 3:22).

Chapter 12

ENDURE DIVINE DISCIPLINE
Hebrews 12:1-29

Christians are inspired by the examples of faith on the part of the courageous people highlighted in Hebrews 11. In Hebrews 12 they are told that the ultimate standard for excellence comes by looking carefully at Christ. Believers are also given instructions about how to properly respond to divine discipline which is called *chastening*.

Believers are to note Christ's example of suffering the shame of crucifixion, and then learn to benefit from the suffering and the correction which we receive. God loves us even when adversity comes. Instead of becoming fearful and upset, we must believe that hard places in life are evidences that God has good purposes for us.

1. The Example of Jesus (12:1-2)

In these verses the Christian life is compared to a foot race. It is a strenuous race[172] which demands perseverance and exhaustion and putting forth much effort.[173] We cannot sit still, or just drift along, in the Christian life.

(12:1-2) Therefore we also, since we are surrounded by so great a cloud of witnesses, let us lay aside every weight, and the sin which so easily ensnares us, and let us run with endurance the race that is set before us, looking unto Jesus, the author and finisher of our faith, who for the joy that was set before Him endured the cross, despising the shame, and has sat down at the right hand of the throne of God.

---

[172] The Apostle Paul often compared the Christian life to a race (1 Corinthians 9:24-26, Galatians 2:2, and Philippians 2:16).

[173] The Greek word translated "race" is *agona*, from which we get "agony."

The Old Testament heroes who had run in the earlier races, have now taken their places in the amphitheater that surrounds the track. They have become a great "cloud of witnesses" (verse 1a). These are not mere spectators, but victors who have run the race before us.

In what sense are *the heroes of faith*, who surround the Christian community, functioning as "so great a cloud of witnesses"? Some understand the "witnesses" to refer to the multitudes of God's faithful followers throughout the ages, who now sit in the stands of eternity—observing God's people today[174] as we seek to live for Christ in the world.

The Christian life is a race to be run. There is an intensity about running; it requires energy. In the race of life, we cannot afford to be hindered by "every weight" and "the sin"[175] that easily entangles us. We are to throw off everything that weighs us down.

Weights are not outright sins, but things that hinder free movement. A "weight" is anything that takes away spiritual sensitivity in our hearts. The Greek word *onkos* speaks of unnecessary hindrances, such as self-pity, lack of discipline, weariness, carelessness, and self-centeredness.

The word "sin" (Greek, *euperistatos*) speaks literally of "entangling sin"—including those acts and attitudes which

---

[174] Wayne Grudem comments about the "cloud of witnesses" in Hebrews 12:1, and says that the text suggests *"that those who have died and gone before, have some awareness of what is going on in the earth. Scripture says very little about this, probably because it does not want us to speak to those who have died, or pray to them, or to contact them in any way...nonetheless, Hebrews 12:1-2 does give us this slight hint, probably as an encouragement to us to continue also to be faithful to God as were those who have died and gone to heaven before us"* (*Systematic Theology*, pages 820-821).

[175] In our day sin is looked upon lightly. In television shows and in commercial movies—the characters rebel against the moral laws of God, but are portrayed to live happily ever after. There is a perfume called "My Sin." One would never guess that sin is a stench in the nostrils of God.

are offensive to God—such as unbelief, worry, bitterness, drunkenness, sexual immorality, and prayerlessness.[176]

Jesus is the "author" and "finisher" of our faith (verse 2). He is the *author*—in the sense of being our Captain, the One from whom we take orders. He is the *finisher*—in the sense of being the One who perfects, the One who seeks to round out and mature our characters. On the cross of Calvary, Jesus both began and finished the actual work of redemption, propitiation, and reconciliation.

The "joy that was set before Him"[177] most likely refers to the glory that He had with the Father before the world was, but which He now exchanged for the cross and the shame that accompanied it. However, after His work of salvation was finished, He looked forward to sitting down again in the presence of God the Father.

When the going gets difficult we are to look to Jesus as a model of endurance and perseverance (verse 2).

2. The Discipline of God (12:3-11)

The major Bible teaching on chastisement is found in these verses. Some form of the word "chastening" appears nine times in this passage.

Chastening involves the discipline and correction of the child of God. The writer of Hebrews wants to show the blessings that discipline can bring to the genuine Christian. He compares the discipline practiced by our earthly fathers to discipline used by our heavenly Father.

---

[176] There is some reason for believing that the singular "the sin" refers to one particular sin—a failure to maintain a stick-to-it-tive-ness for Christ and the church—losing heart and not persevering when the going gets difficult.

[177] The "joy that was set before Him" might also refer to the anticipation of seeing the salvation of lost men and women. Isaiah wrote about Jesus, and said, "He shall see of the travail of his soul, and shall be satisfied" (KJV, Isaiah 53:11).

a) Consider Christ's suffering (12:3-4)

(12:3-4) For consider Him who endured such hostility from sinners against Himself, lest you become weary and discouraged in your souls. You have not yet resisted to bloodshed, striving against sin.

The emphasis in verse 3 is on the tremendous cost of the Christian faith. It cost the life of the Son of God. And if Christians will think about the hostility that Jesus had endured, even to the point of shedding blood, they will see that their difficulties in strenuously running the race of life are mild by comparison.

We are not to grow weary and lose heart as we run the Christian race. William Barclay points out that early writers used the words "weary and discouraged" (verse 3b) to describe the athlete who flings himself on the ground, almost at the point of collapse after he has surged past the finish line.

Instead of becoming weary in the race, we are to "consider" Jesus Christ and the shame that He endured. If we will thoughtfully think about the sufferings of Christ, it will make our own suffering seem meager. The early Christians had experienced mockery and ridicule and economic pressure, but the writer implies that they sooner or later might experience actual bloodshed (verse 4).[178]

The child of God, no matter what his setting, has not suffered to the same extent that Christ suffered (verse 4), for down through the years most Christians have not suffered martyrdom ("resisted to bloodshed").

Scripture teaches that Christians can rejoice in their sufferings, for the Lord disciplines those whom He loves.

---

[178] Many Christians experienced bloodshed. For a book telling the stories of Anabaptist martyrs from the sixteenth century, read *"In the Whale's Belly"* by James W. Lowry. The book is written at a children's level and is a simple telling of some of the incidents recorded in the 1,000-page *Martyrs Mirror*.

b) Accept chastisement graciously (12:5-6)

(12:5-6) And you have forgotten the exhortation which speaks to you as to sons: "My son, do not despise the chastening of the LORD, nor be discouraged when you are rebuked by Him; for whom the LORD loves He chastens, and scourges every son whom He receives."

In these two verses the writer of Hebrews quotes from Proverbs 3:11-12. Christians are to take the Lord's discipline seriously, for when He rebukes, He does it because He loves us. Human discipline is sometimes defective, but the Lord's discipline has to do with maturity and growth.

The word "chastening" is not altogether identical with either *punishment* or *suffering*. There is no one English word that conveys the exact meaning of the Greek *paideia*. The word includes the whole process of training a child, including not only punishment for wrongdoing, but also instruction and encouragement to right behavior.

Chastening from the Lord comes in many forms. The Lord's discipline may include *loss of possessions*, *departure of a loved one*, *serious injury*, *chronic illness*, *unemployment*, *dealing with difficult employers*, and *persecution*. These kinds of problems can bring mental anguish, physical pain, and deep disappointment. The important thing for believers to remember is that the Lord never makes a mistake.

We are not to *"despise"* (detest) the chastening of the Lord (verse 5), nor are we to merely *"endure"* (grit our teeth and bear it—verse 7), but we are to be *"trained"* ("exercised by it" KJV—verse 11). God uses discipline to produce holiness in the lives of His people.

When the Lord disciplines His people, some "despise" the correction (verse 5), but Christians should rejoice in it because God's sovereign hand is at work in their lives. He may well be saying something that is very important.

God's discipline often urges believers to a closer walk with Him. He may teach character qualities by means of troubles—qualities that would not as easily be received if everything went well. In the midst of adversity, there might be a fresh willingness to make new commitments of loyalty to Christ and of love to fellow human beings.

There are two lessons to learn here: *First*, every stroke of discipline administered by the Lord is given in love (verse 6a). It is weighed by Him in fairness, and is designed to suit the believer's needs and to bring healthy change. *Second*, one who receives discipline from the Lord has clear evidence that he is a legitimate "son" (verse 6b).[179]

c) Examine the goals of chastisement (12:7-11)

(12:7-8) If you endure chastening, God deals with you as with sons; for what son is there whom a father does not chasten? But if you are without chastening, of which all have become partakers, then you are illegitimate and not sons.

The point made in verse 7 is that God Himself is educating those who choose to follow Him; the writer employs the illustration of a human father teaching his son.

Modern child training methods have, for the most part, eliminated the rod—but that has not produced better children. Some parents say that they love their children far too much to spank them. Instead, they foolishly coddle them and spoil them so that they become a nuisance to others. Children who are pampered by their parents, later become disrespectful, disobedient, and highly self-centered.

Few children realize it, but in most cases, chastisement is proof that their fathers *care about* what becomes of them. Parents usually punish their children in order to teach them, but not always. Sometimes punishment is inflicted in anger

---

[179] God chastises *sons*; He brings judgment on *sinners*.

or even hatred. Sometimes discipline is all out of proportion to the nature of the offense. God's discipline is fair.

All in God's family receive discipline (verse 8). If any person does not receive chastisement, that person is marked as being an illegitimate child. A "bastard" (KJV) child has no claim to spiritual sonship, or to a spiritual inheritance.

(12:9-11) Furthermore, we have had human fathers who corrected us, and we paid them respect. Shall we not much more readily be in subjection to the Father of spirits and live? For they indeed for a few days chastened us as seemed best to them, but He for our profit, that we may be partakers of His holiness. Now no chastening seems to be joyful for the present, but painful; nevertheless, afterward it yields the peaceable fruit of righteousness to those who have been trained by it.

We have all had human fathers[180] who corrected us, and we "paid them respect" (verse 9a). At first glance, we might expect that discipline would drive a wedge between parent and child—but the opposite is true. The appeal in the latter part of verse 9 is this: *since we have had to submit to human chastening, and have learned to respect our fathers because of their authority—how much more should we be willing to yield to God's discipline and hold Him in awe?*

The "Father of spirits" (verse 9b),[181] disciplines His children; however, His chastisement *is always* administered in love, and always fits the circumstances perfectly. Chastisement is not an evidence of God's displeasure, but an expression of His favor.

Our fathers disciplined us "for a few days" (verse 10) in ways that seemed best to them, but God disciplines us "for

---

[180]   The writer is speaking in general terms. In the 21st century there are many homes where fathers are absent, and there are some children who are orphans.

[181]   The term *Father of spirits* (verse 9) is another description of, and another way of, "expressing the eternal God" (*Christ Above All: The Message of Hebrews*, Raymond Brown,, page 234).

our good" (NIV). With all their best intentions, parents make mistakes. Sometimes they fail to discipline at all, or discipline from wrong motives—and in the wrong way or at the wrong time. God makes no such mistake. He chastens for our good and to draw us closer to Himself.

The actual experience of receiving chastening (verse 11) is not pleasant, but chastening (when done properly) does bring about change. No child enjoys receiving a whipping. The child doesn't say, "I love being paddled; I can't wait for the next whipping." Nobody talks that way. But afterward, for those who submit to its training, it yields the peaceable fruit of righteousness to those "trained by it" (verse 11b).

In summary, the writer discusses *why* Christians are chastised.[182] Chastening is an educational process (verse 10); it is proof of God's genuine love (verse 6); it helps train for obedience (verse 9); it produces uprightness in the life of the individual (verse 11). The trials which God the Father allows to come our way—when accepted properly—*deepen* our understanding, *enlarge* our sympathies, *strengthen* our faith, *stabilize* our purpose, *mellow* our attitudes, and *make us* more Christ-like in character.

The Christian should consider discipline a blessing and a cause for joy, because it has so many positive outcomes in

---

[182] D. L. Moody used to tell of a wealthy couple whose only child died as a baby. The parents were broken-hearted. They tried to fill up the void in their lives by taking a trip to the Holy Land. It was there that they saw a shepherd who was trying to coax some sheep across a stream—but the fast-running water frightened the sheep and they held back, refusing to cross. Finally, the shepherd stooped down and took a lamb, and carried it across the river. The mother sheep watched her baby lamb being taken away—and suddenly she lost her fear of the stream. Very soon, she followed the shepherd, and soon the whole flock was on the other side. *That incident spoke to the bereaved parents and helped them realize what God was doing in their lives. He was taking their little lamb and using that experience to help them loosen their grip on this world, with its fleeting pleasures, and making eternity and Heaven much more real to them.*

the realm of Christian growth and in our relationship with the heavenly Father.

Verse 10 is a reminder that parents train a child "for a few days." Children soon grow up, leave home, and move beyond the discipline of their parents. God, by way of contrast, disciplines us for a lifetime. He disciplines us for our good that we may share in His holiness.

3. The Necessity of Obedience (12:12-17)

These verses contain some practical admonitions; some of the statements are symbolic of great truths. The "hands" are a metaphor for *service*. The "knees" are a picture of *attitudes*. The "feet" symbolize the Christian's *daily walk*.

a) Be strong and keep a straight path (12:12-13)

(12:12-13) Therefore strengthen the hands which hang down, and the feeble knees, and make straight paths for your feet, so that what is lame may not be dislocated, but rather be healed.

Drooping hands and tired knees are marks of a person who is utterly exhausted. The appeal is to look to Jesus, and receive an incentive to let our hands be extended out to the needy, and let the knees cease to tremble with fear. God's people are to stand up firmly like men.

It is important for every Christian to walk carefully day after day, for we are examples to others who notice our testimony. Each must think in these terms: *someone younger than you, weaker than you, may be following you.*

b) Live in peace and pursue holiness (12:14-17)

(12:14-17) Pursue peace with all people, and holiness, without which no one will see the Lord: looking carefully lest anyone fall short of the grace of God; lest any root of bitterness springing up cause trouble, and by this many become defiled; lest there be any fornicator or profane person like

Esau, who for one morsel of food sold his birthright. For you know that afterward, when he wanted to inherit the blessing, he was rejected, for he found no place for repentance, though he sought it diligently with tears.

The word "pursue" ("follow," KJV)[183] conveys the idea that living peaceably with others, and in holiness before God, are indispensable ingredients for an authentic Christian life.

To pursue "peace with all people" (verse 14a) is a mandate of the Scriptures. It was one of the major points of Anabaptist belief and practice. We are not to seek peace to the extent of compromising clear biblical convictions, but neither are God's people to be cantankerous and the kinds of persons who are difficult to live with.

There are some practical rules for making peace:

1) Resolve to be humble in attitude. We must meet hostile people with an overflowing spirit of good will. We must become tender, teachable, and Christ-like.

2) Pray that God will bring change. We should pray, asking the Lord specifically to help us find ways for getting along better with family members, with the boss at work, with obnoxious people, and with other persons in the church.

3) Try to see the other person's point of view. We get into trouble when we expect others to be just like we are. Our bodily constitutions differ; temperaments differ. Peter was an outspoken man; Andrew was a quiet man; two of the disciples were "sons of thunder;" yet each had a significant part to play in God's plan.

4) Guard carefully the use of the tongue. The tongue is in the mouth; it's in a wet place; it is easy to let it slip.

5) Learn the art of communicating charitably. Instead of losing tempers, raising voices, and pounding fists—we are to kindly approach the offending person and try to become reconciled.

6) Practice forbearance and forgiveness. Forbearance means to "hold everything back." Forgiveness means to "hold nothing against."

---

[183]   The Greek word *dioko*, means *to seek eagerly, to earnestly endeavor* to live peaceably with others and to manifest an intensity of purpose to live a life that is marked by holiness. Believers cannot *coast along* on their way to Heaven.

Both qualities are to be practiced in the Christian life (Colossians 3:13).

7) *Acknowledge that some conflict may not disappear.* We are to "live peaceably with all men" (Romans 12:18), but only "as much as depends on you." This qualifying statement implies that sometimes it is not possible to get along absolutely harmoniously with all persons. If we try to reconcile differences, and the other person does not cooperate, we may have to accept the fact that (at least for now), the tension will continue. But don't give up; keep on trying to get along with the critic.

To *pursue peace* does not mean that we must surrender biblical convictions, but it does mean that we will be courteous, considerate, and willing to comply with legitimate social customs, and that we will refuse to quarrel.

To pursue "holiness" (verse 14a) means to strive to follow God's standards rather than the world's standards[184] for right living. Holiness speaks of an internal change that brings the mind, affections, and will into harmony with the Word of God. It means that the believer's ideals and aims will be different from those who live for this life only. It is not that persons here in this life will attain absolute holiness,[185] but one who earnestly keeps on desiring it, and by

---

[184]   In 1572, an Anabaptist believer, just before his death, wrote a letter to his only daughter. This is a portion of his letter: "Read the Holy Scriptures, and when you have attained your years, ponder it well…so that you shall be able to discern good from evil, lies from truth, and the narrow way that leads to eternal life. When you see pomp, boasting, dancing, lying, cheating, cursing, quarreling, fighting, and other wickedness…think then, that this is not the right way. Diligently search…and you will find the little flock who follow Christ. They lead a penitent life; they avoid that which is evil; they delight in doing what is good; they are not conformed to the world; they crucify their sinful flesh more and more every day…they do evil to no one; they pray for their enemies; they do not resist their enemies…" (John C. Wenger, *Separated unto God*, page 68).

[185]   The Anabaptists were noted for stressing holiness in one's daily life, and they were sometimes in danger because they did not curse, or drink to excess, or abuse their family members. The Mennonite historian, C. J. Dyck, says that, "Because he does not swear and because he leads an inoffensive life—therefore men suspect Hans Jager of [being linked with] Anabaptism" (*An Introduction to Mennonite History*, page 312). Jager was thought to be an Anabaptist because he did not swear or quarrel or do other such like things.

the grace of God keeps moving forward in Christian growth, that person will see the Lord (verse 14b).

By deliberate choice, in our daily conduct, we seek cleansing from defilement. We choose those things which make for righteousness. We are careful to "make no provision for the flesh, to fulfill its lusts" (Romans 13:14).

The chief obstacle to holiness is not always opposition from the devil. The chief obstacle for many is inconsistency. Professing Christians often *talk about* perfect love, but at the same time *manifest attitudes* that are narrow, critical, and judgmental in spirit. Such attitudes work against the realization of holiness in one's life.

To "fall short of the grace of God" (verse 15a) is a condition to avoid. In spite of all the warnings in some circles about salvation not being related to "good works," we are to make no mistake about it—*holiness in life* is a very important ingredient in receiving final salvation, which indeed is initiated and achieved only by the grace of God. Those who pursue practical sanctification (holiness in life) prove that they have been saved by the grace of God.

One of the marks of holy living is guarding carefully that no "root of bitterness" lodges in the heart (verse 15b). Bitterness stems from failure to forgive a hurt or an offense against the individual. The phrase "cause trouble" is translated from the Greek *enochlei*, which means "to crowd." Any root of bitterness that springs up within the soil of the human heart will crowd out a sense of thanksgiving.

Another mark of holy living comes from guarding carefully "lest there be any fornicator...like Esau" (verse 16a). Esau married six[186] wives—Judith, Basemath, Adah, Aholibamah, another Basemath, and Mahalath. The state-

---

[186] See under "Esau's wives" in *Nelson's Illustrated Bible Dictionary*, page 351.

ment in verse 16a is a reference to *sexual impurity*,[187] or it may be a symbol of *religious infidelity*.[188]

A "profane person" (verse 16b) is one who has trampled upon a divinely given privilege. Esau was so hungry that he forgot the higher and more important things. The word translated "profane" is *bebelos*, meaning that he was thoroughly consumed with secular things. The NIV translates *bebelos* with the word "godless." Esau sold his birthright for a mere morsel of food.

The "birthright" (verse 16b) carried with it a number of special privileges: first, the recipient became chief over the entire family. Second, he received a double portion of the father's estate. And third, he came into the genealogical line leading to the birth of Christ. Esau, however, rejected the faith of his father and grandfather, and despised his birthright. Esau scoffed at sacred things. He did not count his birthright as a sacred blessing. The pleasure of satisfying his physical hunger was more important than his birthright.

The writer of Hebrews then goes on to describe what happened later to Esau, as given in the book of Genesis, when Jacob stole Esau's birthright (Genesis 27:1-40). The writer of Hebrews says that Esau "afterward, when he wanted to inherit the blessing…was rejected, for he found no place for repentance" (verse 17). Esau shed tears when he

---

[187] Esau was brought up in the godly home of Isaac and Rebekah, but he deliberately decided to live a life that brought grief to his parents. He married two Canaanite women. That was distressful to Isaac and Rebekah (Genesis 26:34-35). When Esau saw his father's grief, he married a daughter of Ishmael, the son of Abraham (Genesis 28:9). It is not certain what Isaac thought about Esau's marrying into the family of Ishmael.

[188] Louis Evans thinks that the author "is speaking metaphorically, and that while the word *pornos* can mean a male prostitute…it is possible to think of Esau as prostituting himself to his passionate desire for food, so that he was willing to give a long-term promise for the immediate gratification of a single morsel of food offered by Jacob" (*The Communicator's Commentary: Hebrews*, page 232).

realized that he had squandered his birthright, but his tears were futile. It was too late to reverse his foolish actions.

Sometimes young persons lose their virginity when caught up in physical touching. The hormones are raging and they go much farther than they intended to go in the physical relationship. Although they may repent, and God may forgive them, they can never again recapture their God-given purity and innocence. They must live with the results of their foolish actions throughout life.

There are some choices in life that can never be reversed. Once made, they must stand.

4. The Two Contrasting Mountains (12:18-24)

The author of Hebrews now gives the ultimate reason why *the attitude of a Christian* is fundamentally different from that of a man like Esau.

There is a fundamental difference of spirit that characterizes the old covenant and the new covenant. The old covenant had been given at Sinai under terrifying conditions. The description of the conditions in verses 18-21 are quotes from the Septuagint translation of Exodus 19.

In this section of Hebrews 12, the old covenant (the law) and the new covenant (the gospel), are contrasted by comparing Mount Sinai (where the law was given), with Mount Zion (where the temple in Jerusalem was located). It was in the temple on Mount Zion that animal sacrifices taught about God's mercy, and it was on Mount Zion where Jesus was crucified, and the message of God's grace became possible. There is a real contrast between the *terrified* approach to God which people in Old Testament times experienced, and the *joyful* approach to God that believers in Christ experience in New Testament times.

a) The earthly mountain (12:18-21)

(12:18-21) For you have not come to the mountain that may be touched and that burned with fire, and to blackness and darkness and tempest, and the sound of a trumpet and the voice of words, so that those who heard it begged that the word should not be spoken to them anymore. (For they could not endure what was commanded: "And if so much as a beast touches the mountain, it shall be stoned or shot with an arrow." And so terrifying was the sight that Moses said, "I am exceedingly afraid and trembling.")

Mount Sinai "burned with fire" (verse 18) at the time when God descended to give the Ten Commandments (recorded in Exodus 19:18). It was wrapped with darkness caused by a thick cloud that covered the mountain. There was a "tempest" (verse 18) which was accompanied by thunder, lightning, and an earthquake (Exodus 19:16-18).

The people asked that Moses speak to them, rather than that God should speak directly to them (Exodus 20:19). The mountain at Sinai was not to be touched by man or beast, under the penalty of death (verse 20). Even Moses trembled, frightened by the terrible display of God's power and holiness (verse 21).

The law given at Sinai was designed to state the holy requirements necessary to achieve God's favor, and to create an awareness of fear if the laws were not kept. The law did not provide a gracious means by which condemned sinners would be drawn into the presence of God.

b) The heavenly mountain (12:22-24)

(12:22-24) But you have come to Mount Zion and to the city of the living God, the heavenly Jerusalem, to an innumerable company of angels, to the general assembly and church of the firstborn who are registered in heaven, to God the Judge of all, to the spirits of just men made perfect, to Jesus the Mediator of the new covenant, and to the blood of

sprinkling that speaks better things than that of Abel.

The clause, "But you have come to Mount Zion and to the city of the living God" (verse 22), is an introduction to the blessings and realities of the new covenant.

The heavenly mountain (Mount Zion) is the site of the city of Jerusalem (John 12:12-15; Romans 11:26). Mount Zion also refers to the "heavenly Jerusalem." Just as the earthly Jerusalem was the center of the political and religious life for Israel in New Testament times, so the heavenly city will be the future seat of divine government.

The terrifying demonstration associated with the old covenant, is here contrasted with the heavenly fellowship of the church—in which saints who live on earth, the spirits of the departed redeemed ones, and hosts of angels (verses 22b-23) are in sweet and mystic communion and fellowship around the throne of God.

In this section of the epistle, the writer of Hebrews was thinking not only of the contrast between Old Testament times and New Testament times, but he was also looking forward to the heavenly Jerusalem.

5. *Fifth Warning Passage—danger of stubborn refusal (12:25-29)*

In this final section of Hebrews 12, the writer of the letter lifts up the Word of God as a message from heaven with which every human being must deal. The Word of God must either be received and obeyed or rejected as unworthy of giving any consideration.

(12:25-29) See that you do not refuse Him who speaks. For if they did not escape who refused Him who spoke on earth, much more shall we not escape if we turn away from Him who speaks from heaven, whose voice then shook the earth; but now He has promised, saying, "Yet once more I shake not only the earth, but also heaven." Now this, "Yet

once more," indicates the removal of those things that are being shaken, as of things that are made, that the things which cannot be shaken may remain. Therefore, since we are receiving a kingdom which cannot be shaken, let us have grace, by which we may serve God acceptably with reverence and godly fear. For our God is a consuming fire.

The command is clear: "See that you do not refuse Him who speaks" (verse 25).[189] We are to recognize and obey the voice of God. At Sinai, *Moses* served as mediator between God and man. Moses was the intermediary with respect to the covenant God made with man. But Sinai represents that which is temporary. God replaced the old covenant with a new covenant, and *Jesus* became the Mediator of it. Readers now, are not to look to Moses, but to Jesus.

It would be folly to do as Esau did—and trade something of immense value for something which is meager and could never satisfy. It would surely *not be wise* to trade the sweet and gentle blessings of the Christian faith, for the cold, hard, formal, and unsatisfying practices of Judaism.

When God spoke through Moses at Sinai, the earth shook. There is coming a day in the future when God will shake both heaven and earth—and only the unshakable things will be left. Among the unshakable things is the eternal kingdom of God (verses 26-28a). There are other things that cannot be shaken—including God's eternity, God's promises, God's Word, and God's love.

The reminder in verse 28b is that God's people are to show gratitude by *serving* God "acceptably" with reverence and awe. Enoch is an example of a person who served God

---

[189] Brethren writer, L. W. Teeter, says, "The superiority of Christ (who came from heaven), over Moses (who was but a man of the earth)—makes the message of Christ so much greater than that of Moses; and especially because Moses was only a type of Christ…it is impossible for those who turn away from Christ to escape punishment." (*New Testament Commentary, Volume 2*, pages 407-408).

acceptably. He walked with God and pleased Him, and was commended for his faith (Hebrews 11:5). Enoch's life was pleasing to God because he was a man of righteousness; as a result "God took him" so that he did not experience death.

Just as Enoch was careful to please God—so we, out of a deep sense of appreciation for the favor bestowed upon us by our heavenly Father—should give back to Him our glad and joyful service. We should fling ourselves wholeheartedly into serving God. Jesus *served* by washing Peter's feet, eating with outcasts, touching lepers, and healing the sick.

Nothing in the letter to the Hebrews teaches that the Christian life is easy. The Christian life is like a long distance run; it takes sustained effort. Believers are to hold on to grace, and offer well-pleasing service to God, obeying Him with a sense of deep respect.

The race is challenging; God's discipline is sometimes unpleasant. The dangers that accompany the race include a bitter spirit, and the foolish trampling upon divinely given privileges, such as the birthright which Esau tossed aside for the temporary pleasures of this life.

Reverence and awe are linked with the fact that our God "is a consuming fire" (verse 29). *Fire* is a symbol of God's *holiness*. This aspect of God's character must be remembered, especially in a day when many stress only the *grace* of God. The true and living God is the One who will eventually burn up all that is unfit to abide in His presence.

The Voice *which now appeals*, urging that we come boldly to the throne of grace to find help in time of need, will one day *issue a shout* that calls the dead from their graves, and sends the earth reeling to destruction. He will then establish an everlasting Kingdom which cannot be moved.

Chapter 13

EXHORTATIONS TO CHRISTIAN LIVING
Hebrews 13:1-25

The closing chapter of Hebrews shows the loving relationship between the writer and his readers. The author first gives admonitions about social duties. Those who believe are to show love for their brethren, hospitality to strangers, concern for prisoners, and loyalty to one's married partner.

Religious duties are spelled out in the next part. There must be respect for elders, guarding against false teaching, and bearing the reproach of Christ. Some personal instructions are given at the very end of the chapter. These include a request for prayer for the writer, prayer for the readers, and some final greetings in the last two verses.

1. Communal Obligations (13:1-6)

The epistle closes with a series of practical commands. The Christian life, lived in the power of the Holy Spirit, is to be a means of blessing and encouragement to others.

a) Loving the brethren (13:1)

(13:1) Let brotherly love continue.

The command to show love for fellow believers is simple and direct. The phrase "brotherly love" is translated from the Greek word *philadelphia*.[190] The Apostle John explains that those believers who are possessed with brotherly love have "passed from death to life" (1 John 3:14).

---

[190] The word "philadelphia" comes from *phileo*, which is one of several words we translate "love," meaning human affection, kindness, and friendship. It is not the same as *agape*, which is a God-like, self-sacrificing love. When phileo is taken together with adelphos, it means "brotherly love"—literally persons born from the same womb. Brothers in Christ have been born from the same source.

The world in which we live is teeming with hostility between persons, and so love for others within the Christian community, marks out those who serve a different Master.

In spite of this biblical command, the greatest hostility that many Christians have experienced in life, has come from other Christians who have become bitter and calloused, instead of being tender and compassionate. Brotherly love is a tender plant that needs lots of attention. It quickly wilts under the frost of harsh words and critical attitudes.

b) Entertaining strangers (13:2)

(13:2) Do not forget to entertain strangers, for by so doing some have unwittingly entertained angels.

In earlier times, inns were places of ill repute. Christians were to open their homes to travelers, and to show them the love of Christ. The grace of hospitality was especially appreciated. Today the need for hospitality continues. It is a blessing to have homes in our congregations where visiting evangelists and missionaries are always welcome.

The phrase "entertain strangers" is the translation of the word *philoxenia*, meaning "lover of strangers"—and a lover of strangers, over the years, has come to mean hospitality. A hospitable person is a warm, gracious individual whose heart and home are open to others. Hospitable persons enjoy meeting new persons and having visitors in their home. Happy and unexpected results may follow hospitality.

We are not to extend warm hospitality *only* to our immediate circle of friends, but to "strangers" as well. Hospitality is to be shown to outsiders as well as to insiders. The assembly of Christians that shows love to strangers will soon have plenty of strangers to love.

The fact that some "have unwittingly (*unawares*, KJV) entertained angels" most likely refers to Abraham's experience as recorded in Genesis 18:1-8.

c) Remembering prisoners (13:3)

(13:3) Remember the prisoners as if chained with them—those who are mistreated—since you yourselves are in the body also.

A number of early Christians were imprisoned[191] because of their faith in Christ. The need for remembering prisoners was especially important. Those who simply proclaimed that they are Christians discovered that such a testimony was a cause for imprisonment in early centuries.

Prisons were usually miserable, damp dungeons dug out under government buildings. It is only in recent centuries that prisons provided ample food, shelter, and medical care for those who were incarcerated. People in prison have time to think and are often open to the gospel message.

Some of our own neighbors may be suffering from a variety of forms of imprisonment—the elderly, shut-ins, and widows who have long evenings and lonely weekends. It is not enough just to feel sorry for such people; we must hurt with them, share their affliction, and feel their pain.

d) Honoring marriage vows (13:4)

(13:4) Marriage is honorable among all, and the bed undefiled; but fornicators and adulterers God will judge.

Marriage is the institution whereby a man and a woman are joined together in the legal relationship of husband and wife. Marriage was established by God when He created the first human pair (Genesis 2:20-24). It is the foundation upon which the family and society are built.

The writer of Hebrews exalts marriage and calls for sexual purity. Marriage is to be held in honor because it is a divinely ordained relationship. The Christian attitude toward

---

[191] Simon Kistemaker suggests that we should expand the concept "*prisoner* to include the shut-ins and the elderly who are confined to a bed, a hospital room, or a private home" (*New Testament Commentary*: Hebrews, page 412).

marriage includes a commitment to purity and a rejection of the idea that marriages can be dissolved[192] whenever either one of the partners chooses.

The marriage relationship is to be preserved in purity; those who violate the marriage covenant will most certainly have to face God regarding their sin. God will deal severely with those who violate His standard for marriage, family, and the home. The text clearly says that "fornicators[193] and adulterers God will judge."

There is only one type of sexual pleasure that is blessed by God—and that is the relationship between a man and a woman within an honorable marriage bond. All other sexual pleasure is prohibited by God, and will defile the hearts of persons who violate His laws. Unrepentant persons who live in serial adultery or fornication are under the wrath of God and will be judged, no matter how much they boast about having had a salvation experience.[194]

The word "bed" (verse 4) here is a symbol for sexual intercourse, and God demands that the relationship be kept within honorable marriage. Fornication and adultery are very wicked sins, not even to be named among the people of God (Ephesians 5:3). The idea that sex is a "right" and can be performed with whoever is available and willing—is far removed from the high standard approved by God.

---

[192]   God recognizes the original marriage of a man and a woman as being valid. If there is a divorce and the first partner is still living, God calls the second marriage "adultery." For more on family breakups and divorce and remarriage, see the *BNTC Commentary on Matthew*, pages 68-70 and pages 230-234.

[193]   In the sea of paganism around us, sexual immorality is rampant. Even among God's people fornication, adultery, incest, sexual abuse, and pornography are more common than is often acknowledged. Provocative behavior in the culture tends to rub off on professing Christians who get many of their cues for living from the various media. Moral purity is necessary for strong marriages and healthy families. Marriage is to be heterosexual and indissoluble (Genesis 2:24).

[194]   See *Hebrews, Volume 2*, R. Kent Hughes, pages 218-219.

God intended marriage to be a life-long relationship. Vows and agreements made at the time of marriage, are made before God and human witnesses, and therefore are to be honored as being most sacred (Matthew 19:6).

Marriage is only for this life (Matthew 22:30), but the intimacy and love and beauty and mutual joy within marriage make it a fitting symbol of the eternal union between Christ and the church (Ephesians 5:21-32).

e) Maintaining contentment (13:5-6)

(13:5-6) Let your conduct be without covetousness; be content with such things as you have. For He Himself has said, "I will never leave you nor forsake you." So we may boldly say: "The LORD is my helper; I will not fear. What can man do to me?"

Jesus spoke about the deceitfulness of wealth and mentioned how the desire for things will sometimes come in and choke out the word of God (Mark 4:19).

The word *covet* speaks of undue desire.[195] The Scriptures do not forbid owning a house, buying a car, or eating good food. What is forbidden is an obsessive, compulsive, lusting after those things, especially luxurious things. There is also a positive kind of coveting. We *should covet* "the best gifts" (1 Corinthians 12:31). We *are to covet* a good name, a sweet spirit, and a Christ-like character.

Verses 5-6 are a warning against the improper love of money. Like the Apostle Paul, it is important for believers to *learn* to be content with what they have (Philippians 4:11). The art of being content is a virtue which Christians must cultivate. Every person comes into this world without a

---

[195] One of the root words translated "covet" means "to boil." It denotes a fervent and passionate desire. It signifies an excessive appetite for wealth and earthly possessions. It is a feeling of always wanting more. Jeremiah was inspired to say that every individual person "is given to covetousness" (Jeremiah 6:13).

penny in his pocket (in fact, without a pocket to put a penny in), and we will leave this world without taking any material goods along into the next stage of life. The Bible attaches great significance to money and its use. It is not only a form of wealth and a medium of exchange, but how persons use it is an index to the character of those who possess it.[196]

The term "without covetousness" (Greek, *aphilargyros*) means "without love of money."[197] Those who are satisfied with fewer things and more quietness are generally happier than those who seek more. The key to being content with limited material goods, is to really believe the Lord's promise, "I will never leave you nor forsake you" (verse 5b). True contentment comes from resting in God's care.

---

[196] Corrie ten Boom recounts an event from her childhood that well illustrates the power of keeping money in perspective. The ten Boom family prayed one morning that God would send a customer that day to the family's shop to purchase a watch. They would use the income to pay bills that had come due at the bank. During that day a customer with a large sum of cash came into the store, picked out, and paid for an expensive watch. At the same time he complained about a Christian watchmaker who he claimed had sold him a defective watch. Casper, Corrie's father, asked the man if he could examine the watch that was not working properly—and he discovered that only a minor repair was needed. Casper repaired the watch, and assured the customer that he had really been sold a fine quality watch that would work well for him. Then he gave the money back to the astounded man, and the man returned the watch he had just bought.

Little Corrie asked, "Papa, why did you do that? Aren't you worried about the bills you have that are due?" Her father responded, "There is blessed and unblessed money," explaining that God would not be pleased with ruining another believer's reputation. He assured her that God would provide. And just a few days later, another man came into the shop and paid for the most expensive watch available. The purchase not only allowed the family to pay their bills, but also provided funds for Corrie to receive training in Switzerland as a watchmaker (*Living in Light of Eternity*, Stacy and Paula Rinehart, page 103).

[197] Joshua spoke words of assurance when reviewing the law for the people of Israel, as recorded in Deuteronomy 31:6, "Be strong and of good courage, do not fear nor be afraid...for the Lord your God, He is the One who goes with you. He will not leave you nor forsake you." David spoke similar words of assurance to his son Solomon in 1 Chronicles 28:20.

2. Remember Spiritual Leaders (13:7-8)

We are to be mindful of those who were our leaders in times past. Some think it is clever to debunk the past, but rather, it is helpful to sing "Faith of our fathers, living still," and be stirred by their faith and courage.

(13:7-8) Remember those who rule over you, who have spoken the word of God to you, whose faith follow, considering the outcome of their conduct. Jesus Christ is the same yesterday, today, and forever.

The words "those who rule over you"[198] are a reference to the church leaders—especially to the elders of the church, those who "rule well" (1 Timothy 5:17).

Departed faithful church leaders can bless the memory of those who had known them. They can still speak, and often include men from several denominations.[199]

Things here on earth often change. Those who grow up in an area of the country, and then move away—are usually surprised by the many changes that have taken place in the community during their years of separation. But the Bible is clear in stating that *Jesus Christ does not change.*

Earthly leaders come and go, but Jesus Christ is always there. *Yesterday*, in the days of His flesh, He became our Substitute when He died on the cross. *Today*, He is at the right hand of the heavenly Father serving as an Advocate for us. *Tomorrow* He will come as a King to reign over the earth. Every knee will bow and all will confess Him as Lord.

---

[198] The Greek phrase translated "those who rule over you," refers to a *leader*, a governor—especially to one of the functions of a leader, that of ruling.

[199] Some of the Brethren leaders who made a mark on my life were I. N. H. Beahm, D. I. Pepple, Jesse Whitacre, G. Howard Danner, and my father, Noah Martin. Among Mennonite leaders were George R. Brunk, Sanford G. Shetler, and J. C. Wenger. Brethren in Christ leaders include E. J. Swalm and C. N. Hostetter. Those from Protestant groups include J. I. Packer, Vance Havner, Warren Wiersbe, M. R. DeHaan, Howard Hendricks, and George Sweeting.

The Christ who lives in you is the same Christ who had part in bringing the earth into existence, and formed the human brain, and promised a dwelling-place in His presence forever—for those who embrace Him as Savior.

All believers need a reminder that Christ is active and abiding and real—not only yesterday and forever, but *today* as well. Jesus Christ is to be the object and the ongoing focus of our lives. We are to seek to "walk just as He walked."

3. Avoid Strange Teaching (13:9-11)

The Apostle Paul warned the elders at Ephesus that savage wolves would "rise up, speaking perverse things, to draw away the disciples after themselves" (Acts 20:30).

(13:9-11) Do not be carried about with various and strange doctrines. For it is good that the heart be established by grace, not with foods which have not profited those who have been occupied with them. We have an altar from which those who serve the tabernacle have no right to eat. For the bodies of those animals, whose blood is brought into the sanctuary by the high priest for sin, are burned outside the camp.

Some of the readers were being influenced by teachings that were different from what the apostles had been teaching (verse 9), and were contrary to the Word of God. In the early church there were teachers who promoted philosophies that exalted men's ideas. Colosse had to deal with Gnostic philosophers (Colossians 2:8), and Titus was admonished to "appoint elders" who would rebuke deceivers that were subverting whole households (Titus 1:5-13).

The brazen altar at the door of the Holy Place in the tabernacle was the place where the animal sacrifices in Judaism were slaughtered. The high priest carried the blood of animals into the Most Holy Place as a sin offering (on the

Day of Atonement), but the bodies were later burned outside the camp. Just so, Jesus suffered outside the city gate, to make the people holy through His own blood.

And so we have an altar—the cross on which Jesus died as the sacrificial Lamb of God. It is God's grace[200] that saves those who believe in the blood of the cross. The term "those who serve the tabernacle" (verse 10) is a reference to Jewish persons who continue worshiping with the ritual of the Old Testament tabernacle. They have no rights to the "altar" of the cross. The crucified Savior means nothing to them.

Some professing Christians (with a Jewish background) apparently thought they could have the benefits of belief in Jesus, without laying aside their earlier temple rituals which they practiced in their former Jewish faith.

In verses 10-11, the writer repeats a number of concepts that had been explained in earlier parts of the letter, namely in Hebrews 5:3, 7:27, and 9:7. It will be helpful to read the comments on Hebrews 9:7 (pages 108-109 of this commentary, and especially footnote number 113 on page 109).

4. Strive For Holiness (13:12-16)

Jesus suffered when He died on the cross, and we are challenged to boldly identify with Him, willingly bearing the reproach that accompanies identity with Jesus. Sometimes suffering, public insult, and various forms of persecution have to be endured when one becomes a Christian.

(13:12-16) Therefore Jesus also, that He might sanctify the people with His own blood, suffered outside the gate.

---

[200] When a person works an 8-hour day and receives pay for his time, that is a *wage*. When a person competes with an opponent and receives a trophy for his performance, that is a *prize*. When a person receives recognition for his long service on the job, that is an *award*. But when a person is not capable of earning a wage, or deserves no award—yet receives such a gift anyway, that is *grace*.

Therefore let us go forth to Him, outside the camp, bearing His reproach. For here we have no continuing city, but we seek the one to come. Therefore by Him let us continually offer the sacrifice of praise to God, that is, the fruit of our lips, giving thanks to His name. But do not forget to do good and to share, for with such sacrifices God is well pleased.

The writer of Hebrews seeks to show that the death of Jesus answered to the sin offering in all its major points. Just as the blood of the sin offering in Old Testament times was burned "outside the camp" (verse 11), so Jesus suffered outside the gate of the city of Jerusalem.

We are to identify with Jesus in His shame, if we want to be identified with Him in His future kingdom.[201] The writer of Hebrews says that we are not to be ashamed of the reproach that goes along with being a follower of the despised Christ. Verse 13 also includes the idea that Hebrew Christians are to make a clean break with Judaism, and separate entirely to the Lord Jesus for redemption.

Christians "have no continuing city" (verse 14) in this life. It is not that we live in a world detached from the present. We are ambassadors for Christ here in this life (2 Corinthians 5:20), but we are aware of the brevity of life, and often get anxious for our heavenly home.

The Christian life is to be characterized by "the sacrifice of praise to God" (verse 15). In Christ, we have forgiveness;

---

[201] Too many members in our churches today want to be on the inside with the worldly crowd, instead of being on the outside with God's despised few. It is good to remember that the world today continues to be disturbed by the demands of Jesus. His condemnation of sin, His call to holiness, and His way of salvation are not welcome in the minds of the multitudes. Moses counted *the reproach of Christ* greater riches than all the treasures of Egypt (Hebrews 11:26), but only a relatively few have followed his steps. One of the reasons why only ten percent of Brethren men of military age served in alternative service during World War 2 was "the social pressure of the community, family, and friends" (Donald Durnbaugh, *Fruit of the Vine*, pages 474-475).

now we offer a new kind of gift to God, not a *sin* offering, but a *thank* offering. Old Testament saints brought the fruit of their fields for a sacrifice. New Testament believers are to bring the fruit of their lips (praise) as a sacrifice.

Jesus Christ is our great High Priest. He has purchased our redemption. The terror of death is abolished. A home in Heaven lies ahead. When we think about all that Jesus has done, our hearts should swell up with praise. We will want to bless God, praise the Lord, and thank Him for all He has done. A continual praise to God should be "the fruit of our lips" (verse 15). We are to speak about God's salvation, and sing about it, and express praise with our lips.

The writer then urges that Christians do good and share with others (verse 16). Along with *spiritual worship*, and the use of our lips to glorify God, there must also be *spiritual works*, activities which will benefit others. Doing good should be the Christian's way of life. Wholesome deeds, performed out of loyalty to Christ and the Scriptures, are activities with which "God is well pleased" (verse 16).

5. Obey Church Officers (13:17)

Believers are to render to faithful officers in the church, the submission and respect to which they are entitled by virtue of the authority God has given them. The officers include elders, pastors,[202] overseers, preachers, and teachers.

(13:17) Obey those who rule over you, and be submissive, for they watch out for your souls, as those who must give account. Let them do so with joy and not with grief, for that would be unprofitable for you.

---

[202] William Beahm explains that the word "pastor" is an excellent term which means "shepherd," but that in New Testament times it did not designate a church *office*. "This function came later to be one of the characteristic *offices* of the Christian ministry" (*Studies in Christian Belief*, page 238-239).

Preachers are not super-human, but are weak and unable to carry out most responsibilities in their own strength. They need the moral support and the prayer support of the people in their congregations. The preacher's task is heavy and members of the congregation should not add to the weighty burdens that he bears.

Verse 17 stresses the need to "obey" spiritual leaders, that is, "those who rule over you." The word "obey" means "to assent to another's direction." One may not always agree with his leaders; he may even discuss a disagreement, but subordination to spiritual leaders is necessary to the welfare of the church. Wherever two or more persons are mutually dependent, one must assume responsibility; others must be subordinate.[203] The church is a body; we are members one of another. To rebel against spiritual leaders, is to despise the One who appointed them.

Elders and church leaders often cry to God daily for wisdom to know how to direct the body of Christians in a proper way. The words "they watch out for your souls" (verse 17a) means that faithful elders minister the truth of the gospel in order to build spiritual maturity in the congregation, and sometimes burn midnight oil to prepare good food for the sheep, while his flock is asleep.[204]

Spiritual leaders "watch out for your souls, as those who

---

[203] The obligation to obey does not extend to anything that is wrong. The Bible, for example, says: "O My people! Those who lead you cause you to err, and destroy the way of your paths" (Isaiah 3:12b). Also, Jesus spoke about "blind leaders of the blind" and both falling into the ditch (Matthew 15:14). Also, it is important for elders and church leaders to be reminded they are not to be "lords over those entrusted to [them], but [to be] examples to the flock" (1 Peter 5:3).

[204] There are many questions that arise about particular situations which demand remedies that are not prescribed by specific answers in the Bible. These are often matters about which sincere Christians will disagree. The church officers are often called upon to help settle controversies that arise in the church.

must give account." Genuine preachers are borne down with a heavy burden, because they care *for the souls* of those who are part of the congregation. Their concern for our spiritual welfare is pressing upon them. And the minister who does his work *with the day of accounting in view*—is not a man to be trifled with! It will not pay to take lightly his instructions, exhortations, pleadings, and rebukes.

The words "that would be unprofitable for you" (verse 17b) mean that those who haughtily criticize their leaders are really hurting themselves. Rebellious church members may cause their pastors and elders and deacons to groan because of their bitter criticism—but the rebels themselves will eventually do more than groan. The word "unprofitable"[205] is a strong word that can speak of a sin that leads to eternal perishing.

6. Conclusion: Final Greetings (13:18-25)

The conclusion of the epistle includes personal notes. There is a call to pray, the giving of a beautiful benediction, and some news about Timothy.

(13:18-25) Pray for us; for we are confident that we have a good conscience, in all things desiring to live honorably. But I especially urge you to do this, that I may be restored to you the sooner. Now may the God of peace who brought up our Lord Jesus from the dead, that great Shepherd of the sheep, through the blood of the everlasting covenant, make you complete in every good work to do His will, working in you what is well pleasing in His sight, through Jesus Christ, to whom be glory forever and ever. Amen. And I appeal to you, brethren, bear with the word of exhortation, for I have written to you in few words. Know that our brother Timothy has been set free, with whom I shall see you if he comes shortly.

---

[205] The Greek word is *alusiteles*, literally meaning "chained; not to be loosed."

Greet all those who rule over you, and all the saints. Those from Italy greet you. Grace be with you all. Amen.

In verses 18-19 the writer calls upon his readers to pray for him.[206] He had a "good conscience" which is the result of a cleansed heart and a sincere faith (1 Timothy 1:5). His goal was to live with integrity. He may have lived at a distance, and hoped to be able to return to his readers very soon.

Verses 20-21 contain a benediction that in its first part summarizes what God *has done* in Christ,[207] and the second part reveals what God *is doing now* in the lives of His people. God works in His children that which "is well pleasing in His sight" (verse 21). The writer had asked his readers to pray for him; now this is his prayer for them.

The *first part of the benediction* (verse 20) speaks of our God as a "God of peace" who has resurrection power; He raised "our Lord Jesus from the dead." The "blood of the everlasting covenant" is a reference to "the precious blood of Christ" (1 Peter 1:19) by which He sealed the new covenant with its promises for the people of God.

The *second part of the benediction* (verse 21) speaks of making believers "complete" (perfect, KJV)[208] and has to do

---

[206] Not all can preach effectively, or sing, or go to some field overseas, but all can pray, if their lives are clean and committed. We should pray for those who mistreat us (Matthew 5:44). We should pray for missionaries and soul winners (Matthew 9:38). We should pray for deliverance from temptation (Luke 22:40). We should pray for the salvation of the lost (Romans 10:1). We should pray for wisdom to deal with life's issues (James 1:5). We should pray for the peace of Jerusalem (Psalm 122:6). We should pray for those who minister the Word of God (Ephesians 6:18-19). We should pray about everything (Philippians 4:6).

[207] In the Hebrews 13 benediction, the Lord Jesus is called *the Great Shepherd*. In John 10 He is called *the Good Shepherd* giving His life for the sheep. And in First Peter 5:4 He is *the Chief Shepherd* who one day will appear on earth again, and put an end to life as we know it today.

[208] The Greek term used here is *katartizo*, which means "to strengthen, perfect, complete, make one what he ought to be" (*Thayer's Greek-English Lexicon of the New Testament*, page 336).

with training, disciplining, and equipping for service. The Apostle Paul says that "our sufficiency is from God, who also made us sufficient as ministers of the new covenant" (2 Corinthians 3:5-6). Paul's confidence in preaching was not based on his own abilities, but on what God has done through him. Our natural talents and abilities will only take us so far. Every Christian needs the Holy Spirit's enabling to live a noble life and to serve God honorably.

The writer had more to say, but he tried to be brief (verse 22). The "Timothy" mentioned here (verse 23) is likely the same Timothy who was a companion of Paul. There is no indication to the contrary.

In the last two verses of the letter, the readers were asked to relay the writer's greetings to the church leaders and to the saints in their region (verse 24).

The final words, "Grace be with you all" (verse 25), were the writer's parting wish for his readers. Grace is the wonderful, saving, sustaining, undeserved kindness of God.

The message of Hebrews is that, under the new covenant, we have a better Person—a great High Priest who is engaged in a better priesthood, securing better privileges, which call for better practice in daily living.

The Jewish temple was still standing when Hebrews was written (present tense in Hebrews 10:11), and the elaborate system of animal sacrifices was still in operation. All this beckoned Christians (who were formerly Jews) to forsake Christ and come back into the fold of Judaism. The writer of Hebrews encourages Christians to continue on with Christ. It will be worth it all in the end.

QUESTIONS FOR DISCUSSION
Book of Hebrews

1. What did the writer of Hebrews mean when he declared Jesus to be the radiance of God's glory (1:3)?

2. What are some of the ways that the status of Jesus the Son is seen to be superior to that of the angels (1:4-14)?

3. Why does Jesus merit worship from human beings, even the worship of angels (1:6)?

4. What arguments are used by followers of the cults to reject the deity of Christ? How can they be refuted (1:6-13)?

5. In what ways do angels minister to human beings in our day (1:14)?

6. Name some ways by which it is possible for believers to *neglect* their salvation (2:3).

7. Why do some followers of the Lord Jesus Christ fear death? How can they be helped (2:15)?

8. A Christian nurse who works with critically ill people, is shocked by the decisions of family members to "do everything" to extend people's suffering. She says that such efforts amount almost to causing torture. How do we convince people to let go of their loved ones and entrust them into God's care (2:15)?

9. Notice the way that quotations from the Old Testament Scriptures are introduced (3:7). What do those statements say about the authority of the Bible?

10. When the Israelites were in the wilderness, what did they do (Exodus 17:1-7) that angered the Lord (3:7-11)?

11. What activity among believers is especially important in order to promote spiritual progress (3:13)?

12. What is it that the writer of Hebrews repeatedly warns against, and what do the words mean (4:7; 3:8; 3:15)?

13. In your own words, what does the statement mean, which says, "There remains therefore a rest for the people of God" (4:9)?

14. What are the two exhortations that appear in the words of chapter 4:14-16?

15. List at least three requirements for the high priest, as given in chapter 5:1-4.

16. Comment on the words, "He learned obedience by the things which He suffered" (5:8).

17. Why do you think the writer of Hebrews included the difficult passage in 6:4-8?

18. What other passages in the Bible can you find that link the virtues of faith, hope, and love, as in (6:10-12)?

19. What is signified by the phrase "the Presence behind the veil" (6:19)?

20. Name some of the ways by which Melchizedek was considered "great" (7:3-4).

21. How does one explain that Levi (who lived long after the time of Abraham) paid tithes to Melchizedek (7:9-10)?

22. Make a list of some of the promises that are contained in the new covenant (8:10-12).

23. Describe (giving the approximate size) of each of the three parts that comprised the tabernacle compound (9:1-5).

24. Name some of the events that took place in connection with worship in the tabernacle area (9:6-10).

25. In your own words, seek to explain and apply the sentence which says, "For if we sin willfully…, there no longer remains a sacrifice for sins" (10:26).

26. On what basis do Christians have confidence to enter the innermost sanctuary of God (10:19-21)?

27. Define "faith" in your own words, keeping in mind the teaching in 11:1-3.

28. Can a Christian embrace evolution? If he does accept evolution, does he deny the Genesis record and the meaning of faith (11:3)?

29. What attributes of God must the Christian accept by faith? What features about God do we often find hard to believe?

30. What did Moses value more than the treasures he may have had in Egypt (11:23-31)?

31. Explain why Rahab was spared death; was it because of her faith or her righteousness (11:31)?

32. What do you think is meant in Hebrews 12:1-2, by the term "cloud of witnesses"?

33. Name some of the "weights" that tend to hold back believers from becoming their very best for Christ (12:1).

34. Name some of the "sins" of the saints that wrap themselves tightly around believers and ensnare them (12:1).

35. Name the various responses Christians sometimes give to God's discipline. What are some positive values that come out of chastisement (12:5-11)?

36. Do you think most Christians manifest the virtue of hospitality in our day? Can you distinguish between *entertaining* guests, and *showing hospitality* to visitors (13:2)?

37. Write out your own comments on the teaching about marriage which is found in Hebrews 13:4. List some reasons why marriages fail.

38. Think about some church leaders who had an influence on your early life (13:7). Can you name some of them?

39. Is it your experience that most church members really respect their ministers/pastors (13:17)?

40. What is involved in genuine praise? Is singing a hymn all that is involved in praise? What do you think about the songs that repeat the same words over and over again (13:15)?

SELECTED BIBLIOGRAPHY
Book of Hebrews

Analytical Greek Lexicon. New York: Harper & Brothers, n.d.

Archer, Gleason L. *Encyclopedia of Bible Difficulties*. Grand Rapids: Zondervan Publishing House, 1982.

Archer, Gleason L. *The Epistle to the Hebrews. (Shield Bible Study Series)*. Grand Rapids: Baker Book House, 1957.

Barclay, William. *The Daily Bible Study Series: The Letter to the Hebrews*. Philadelphia: Westminster Press, 1955.

Barnes, Albert. *Barnes' Notes on the New Testament: Hebrews*. Grand Rapids: Baker Book House, 1961.

Beacon Dictionary of Theology, Richard S. Taylor, ed. Kansas City: Beacon Hill Press, 1983.

Beahm, William M. *Studies in Christian Belief*. Elgin, IL: The Brethren Press, 1958.

Bittinger, Emmert F. *Heritage and Promise:Perspectives on the Church of the Brethren*. Elgin, IL: Brethren Press, 1983.

Blough, S. S. *Studies in Doctrine and Devotion* (Kurtz, Blough, Ellis). Elgin, IL:Brethren Publishing House, 1919.

Bowman, Carl F. *Brethren Society: The Cultural Transformation of a Peculiar People*. Baltimore: The Johns Hopkins University Press, 1995.

Bowman, John Wick. *The Layman's Bible Commentary: Hebrews, James, 1 Peter, 2 Peter*. Atlanta: John Knox Press, 1962.

Brown, Raymond. *Christ Above All: The Message of Hebrews*, BST Series. Downers Grove, IL: InterVarsity Press, 1982.

Bruce, F. F. *The Epistle to the Hebrews. (NIC Commentary on the New Testament)*. Grand Rapids: Wm. B. Eerdmans, 1964.

Collins, Owen. *The Classic Bible Commentary*. John Wesley comments on Hebrews. Wheaton, IL: Crossway Books, 1999.

Draper, James T. *Hebrews: The Life that Pleases God*. Wheaton, IL: Tyndale House Publishers, 1976.

Durnbaugh, Donald F. ed. *The Brethren Encyclopedia (3 Volumes)*. Elgin, IL: The Brethren Press, 1983.

Durnbaugh, Donald F. *Fruit of the Vine: A History of the Brethren, 1708 to 1995*. Elgin, IL: Brethren Press, 1997.

Duty, Guy. *If Ye Continue: A Study of the Conditional Aspects of Salvation*. Minneapolis: Bethany Fellowship, Inc., 1966.

Dyck, Cornelius J. *Spiritual Life in Anabaptism*. Scottdale, PA: Herald Press, 1995.

Dyck, C. J. ed. *An Introduction to Mennonite History*. Scottdale, PA: Herald Press, 1967.

Elwell, Walter A., ed. *Evangelical Dictionary of Theology*. Grand Rapids: Baker Book House, 1984.

English, E. Schuyler. *Studies in the Epistle to the Hebrews*. Lancaster, PA: Rudisill & Company, Inc. 1955.

Erickson, Millard J. *Christian Theology*. Grand Rapids, MI: Baker Book House, 1985.

Evans, Louis H. Jr. *The Communicator's Commentary: Hebrews*, Lloyd Ogilvie, ed. Waco, TX: Word Books Publisher, 1985.

Graham, Billy. *Angels: God's Secret Agents (revised and expanded edition)*. Waco, TX: Word Books, 1986.

Greathouse, William M. *Hebrews: Beacon Bible Commentary*. Kansas City, MO: Beacon Hill Press, 1968.

Gromacki, Robert G. *Stand Bold in Grace: An Exposition of Hebrews*. Grand Rapids: Baker Book House, 1984.

Grudem, Wayne. *Systematic Theology*. Grand Rapids: Zondervan Publishing House, 1994.

Guthrie, George H. *The NIV Application Commentary: Hebrews*. Grand Rapids, MI: Zondervan, 1998.

Haldeman, I. M. *The Tabernacle Priesthood and Offerings*. Westwood, NJ: Fleming H. Revell Co., 1925.

Haley, John W. *Alleged Discrepancies of the Bible*. Grand Rapids: Baker Book House, 1874.

Henry, Carl F. H., ed. *The Biblical Expositor, Volume III*. (Berkeley Mickelsen, Hebrews). Philadelphia: A. J. Holman Company, 1960.

Howard, Deborah. *Sunsets: Reflections for Life's Final Journey*. Wheaton, IL: Crossway Books, 2005.

Howard, R. E. *Beacon Bible Commentary: Galatians through Philemon (Volume 9)*. Kansas City, MO: Beacon Hill Press, 1965.

Hughes, R. Kent. *Preaching the Word: Hebrews (2 volumes)*. Wheaton, IL: Crossway Books, 1993.

Ironside, Harry A. *Hebrews and Titus*. New York: Loizeaux Brothers, Inc., Bible Truth Depot, 1932.

Joppie, A. S. *The Ministry of Angels*. Grand Rapids, MI: Baker Book House, 1953.

Kauffman, Daniel, Ed. *Doctrines of the Bible*. Scottdale, PA: Mennonite Publishing House, 1952.

Kent, Homer A., Jr. *The Epistle to the Hebrews*. Grand Rapids: Baker Book House, 1972.

Kistemaker, Simon J. *New Testament Commentary: Hebrews*. Grand Rapids: Baker Book House, 1984.

Lea, Thomas. *Holman New Testament Commentary, Hebrews and James*, Max Anders, ed. Nashville: Broadman & Holman, 1999.

Lockyer, Herbert. *Nelson's Illustrated Bible Dictionary*. Nashville: Thomas Nelson Publishers, 1986.

Lowry, James W. *In the Whale's Belly: Stories of Christian Martyrs*. Harrisonburg, VA: Christian Light Publications, 181,

MacArthur, John. *The MacArthur New Testament Commentary: Hebrews*. Chicago: The Moody Bible Institute, 1983.

MacArthur, John. *The Gospel According to Jesus*. Grand Rapids: Zondervan Publishing House, 1986.

Macaulay, J. C. *Expository Commentary on Hebrews*. Chicago: Moody Press, 1978.

Martin, Harold S. *New Testament Beliefs and Practices: A Brethren Understanding*. Elgin, IL: Brethren Press, 1989.

Meyer, F. B. *An Exposition of the Whole Bible*. Westwood, NJ: Fleming H. Revell Co., 1959.

Meyer, F. B. *The Way into the Holiest: Expositions on Hebrews*. London: Marshall, Morgan & Scott, 1950.

Miller, R. H. *The Doctrine of the Brethren Defended*. Indianapolis: Printing and Publishing House, 1896.

Minutes of the Annual Conference of the Church of the Brethren: 1955-1964, compiled and edited by Ora W. Garber. Elgin, IL: Brethren Press, 1965.

Moore, J. H. *The New Testament Doctrines*. Elgin, IL: Brethren Publishing House, 1915.

Morgan, G. Campbell. *Great Chapters of the Bible*. New York: Fleming H. Revell Co., 1935.

Morris, Henry M. *The Bible and Modern Science*. Grand Rapids: Baker Book House, 1984.

Nead, Peter. *Nead's Theological Works*. Dayton, Ohio: written in 1833; new edition published in 1866.

Nelson's Illustrated Bible Dictionary, Herbert Lockyer, Sr., ed. Nashville, TN: Thomas Nelson Publishers, 1986.

Pettingill, William L. *Into the Holiest: Simple Studies in Hebrews*. Wheaton, IL: Van Kampen Press, 1939.

Pentecost, J. Dwight. *Things to Come*. Findlay, Ohio: Dunham Publishing Compay, 1958.

Pfeiffer, Charles F. *The Epistle to the Hebrews*. (Everyman's Bible Commentary series). Chicago: Moody Press, 1962.

Phillips, John. *Exploring Hebrews*. Chicago: Moody Press, 1977.

Pink, Arthur W. *An Exposition of Hebrews, 3 Volumes*. Grand Rapids, MI: Baker Book House, 1954.

Purkiser, W. T. *Beacon Bible Expositions: Hebrews, James, Peter (Vol. 11)*. Kansas City, MO: Beacon Hill Press, 1974.

Rinehart, Stacy and Paula. *Living in Light of Eternity*. Colorado Springs: Navpress, 1986.

Ross, Robert W. *The Wycliffe Bible Commentary: Hebrews*. Pfeiffer and Harrison, eds. Chicago: Moody Press, 1962.

Shank, Robert. *Life in the Son: A Study of the Doctrine of Perseverance*. Springfield, MO: Westcott Publishers, 1960.

Smith, J. B. *Greek-English Concordance to the New Testament*. Scottdale, PA: Herald Press, 1955.

Spurgeon, Charles. *Spurgeon's Commentary on Great Chapters of the Bible* (compiled by Tom Carter). Grand Rapids: Kregel, 1998.

Stoffer, Dale R. *Background and Development of Brethren Doctrines 1650-1987*. Philadelphia: Brethren Encyclopedia, Inc., 1989.

Stone, Nathan. *Names of God*. Chicago: Moody Press, 1944.

Stone, Nathan J. *Answering Your Questions*. Chicago: Moody Press, 1956.

Taylor, Richard S. *Beacon Bible Commentary*, Volume 10. Kansas City, MO: Beacon Hill Press, 1967.

Teeter, L. W. *New Testament Commentary in Two Volumes*. Mount Morris, IL: The Brethren's Publishing Co., 1894.

Thayer, J. H. *Greek-English Lexicon of the New Testament*. Edinburgh, Scotland, T. & T. Clark, Fourth Ed. 1901.

Thomas, W. H. Griffith. *Hebrews: A Devotional Commentary.* Grand Rapids: Wm. B. Eerdmans Publishing Co., n.d.

Vine, W. E. *The Epistle to the Hebrews: Christ all Excelling.* London: Oliphants Limited, 1952.

Walvoord, John F.; Zuck, Roy B. *The Bible Knowledge Commentary.* New Testament edition. Wheaton, IL: Scripture Press, 1983.

Weaver, J. Denny. *Becoming Anabaptist: The Origin and Significance of 16th Century Anabaptism.* Scottdale, PA: Herald Press, 2005.

Wenger, J. C. *Separated Unto God: A Plea for... a Scriptural Non conformity to the World.* Scottdale, PA: Herald Press, 1955.

Wenger, J. C. *Glimpses of Mennonite History and Doctrine.* Scottdale, PA: Herald Press, 1959.

Wenger, J. C. *Introduction to Theology: Written in the Anabaptist-Mennonite Tradition.* Scottdale, PA: Herald Press, 1954.

Wesley, John. *The Classic Bible Commentary: Hebrews.* Owen Collins, editor. Wheaton, IL: Crossway Books, 1999.

Wiersbe, Warren W. *Be Confident: Hebrews.* Wheaton, IL: Victor Books, 1977.

Wiersbe, Warren W. *Run With the Winners, The Champions of Hebrews 11.* Wheaton, IL: Tyndale House Publishers, 1985.

Winger, Otho. *History and Doctrines of the Church of the Brethren.* Elgin, IL: Brethren Publishing House, 1920.

Wuest, Kenneth S. *Wuest's Word Studies: Hebrews in the Greek New Testament.* Grand Rapids: Wm. B. Eerdmans Publishing, 1953.

(Hebrews 13:20-21) Now may the God of peace who brought up our Lord Jesus from the dead, that great Shepherd of the sheep, through the blood of the everlasting covenant, make you complete in every good work to do His will, working in you what is well pleasing in His sight, through Jesus Christ, to whom be glory forever and ever. Amen.